WILLIAM YEOWARD
THE PERFECT HOST

WILLIAM YEOWARD
THE PERFECT HOST
your entertaining planner

CICO BOOKS
LONDON NEW YORK

Published in 2009 by CICO Books
An imprint of
Ryland Peters & Small
20–21 Jockey's Fields   519 Broadway, 5th Floor
London WC1R 4BW   New York, NY 10012

10 9 8 7 6 5 4 3 2 1

www.cicobooks.com

A CIP catalog record for this book is available from the
Library of Congress and the British Library.

ISBN-13: 978 1 907030 01 7

Printed in China

Designer: Roger Hammond, bluegumdesigners.com
Photographers: Ray Main and Paul Ryan
Additional text: Posy Gentles

Contents

Introduction

For most of us, the very word "entertaining" is enough to send us into a panic! It seems to me that we are so conditioned by the fear of organizing the party that we totally forget that having a gathering is meant to be an enjoyable and fun experience, rather than some alarming endurance course we have set for ourselves. In this journal, I want to illustrate that entertaining is a very broad word for seeing one's friends and family. I love gathering people up from all walks of life for some specific celebration.

To help with the basics, I've included some guidance on choosing china, glassware, cutlery, tablecloths and napkins, flowers and candles—all the elements you need for an attractive and welcoming table. And then there are the themed tables—this section will hopefully inspire you to create memorable table settings for all occasions.

Food is such an important part of entertaining—and I certainly adore cooking—so I have included a selection of favorite recipes: some are classics dishes and some are new ideas. Towards the back of the journal are record pages for you to fill in, with details of your guests and the menu.

I truly love entertaining and hope you will enjoy this book and feel inspired by the hugely varied locations that I have chosen to illustrate my genuine enthusiasm for this age-old occupation.

To close, I should like you to remember two things. Firstly, have fun! Even if it's not fun and you wish you had never invited any of the guests, just pretend! We all have great feelings of doubt just before a party and believe that we are the only people who suffer from this "entertaining anxiety disorder"! It's just not true—all hosts and hostesses frequently have bouts of self doubt but you may be assured that your guests will admire you for making the efforts that you have made and will be keen to reciprocate at the earliest opportunity.

Secondly, when the party's over, sit down and have a good drink and just for a moment reflect on the pleasure that you have given others—it's nice to do that before the washing up!

Good luck!

ETIQUETTE

From sending out the perfect invitation to
compiling the guest list, following a few simple guidelines
will ensure that your party or dinner becomes an event
that your guests will always remember.

Inviting Guests

It is always a thrill when the morning post brings an invitation to a party, to a dinner, or to drinks, rather than just the usual stack of household bills in brown envelopes. So when planning your gathering, send out proper invitations rather than simply picking up the phone or sending an email.

For a formal occasion (or an event to which you wish to invite a large number of people), you could have cards specially printed, but I find it useful to keep a selection of pretty invitation cards (see page 138 for details of my cards), where I can simply fill in the details of the event. You may also like to include a reply card for guests to return to you. If you don't hear back from people, do phone them a few days before the event to check they have actually received the invitation.

When drawing up your guest list, remember that a good mix of people is always preferable because it's so nice for guests when they don't know everyone at a party and nearly everyone enjoys meeting new people.

THE GOOD GUEST

As a guest, you should have responded to your invitation within no more than a week of receiving it. You should dress appropriately and bring a small gift for your host—flowers, champagne, or chocolate are always good choices. Be punctual, but NEVER early. Ten minutes after the time stated on the invitation is considered perfect.

Make a point of thanking your host as you leave. Write a thank-you letter within two days. If you know your host well, an e-mail or telephone call is also welcome as you can chat about the evening.

ETIQUETTE

Inviting Guests
The Art of Greeting
The Dining Table
Spacing and Placing

The Art of Greeting

As people arrive, welcome them at the door, take their coats, and let guests know where the cloakroom is. Furnish them with a drink and then introduce them to a couple of other guests, giving names and a little information about each to get the conversation started. If they are first to arrive, try not to leave them "dangling" in thin air but stay with them and chat.

If you are cooking, prepare as much of the food as you can in advance, so that you can concentrate on looking after your guests. If you are not a natural in the kitchen, then get a cook or a good deli to bring in the food. There's absolutely no point in torturing yourself. Also try to find a good butler—it's well worth it.

Once your guests have all arrived, turn off your mobile phone and put the answer machine on for the house phone, so that you won't be distracted from your role of host or hostess. Your sole focus should be those in your company, not others elsewhere. And, as a guest, switch your phone off on arrival; if you are awaiting an urgent call, turn the phone to vibrate mode rather than ring to avoid disturbing others, and leave the room to take the call.

AT THE TABLE

As a host or hostess, always work out your table plan in advance. In an ideal world, seat your guests between someone they already know and someone they don't, but are likely to find congenial company.

Keep an eye on your table, making sure glasses are topped up and dishes are passed. If you notice conversation is starting to flag, throw in a comment to start it up again. If it's still difficult, move all the men two places to the right after the main course, so everyone has someone new to chat to.

As a guest, you should wait to be seated and start to eat only when your host starts. It is up to you to make conversation and look after your fellow guests by passing them water and wine or whatever it is they need.

It is quite acceptable to leave some food on your plate, but not to make a fuss about not liking a particular dish. If a different wine is served with each course, don't feel obliged to drain the glass each time—a little wasted wine is far preferable to a drunken guest!

The Dining Table

A dining table must be adequate in size for the number of guests you are inviting and for the number of dishes and courses that you intend to serve. A dining chair is usually 20–22in (50–55cm) wide and so is the average place setting. This should help when calculating the number of guests around a table. Ideally, you should try to place everything that you and your guests will need on the table, so there must be sufficient room to accommodate these pieces without the overall effect looking cluttered. If necessary, take a course-by-course approach and only bring to the table what you need for each course and clear it away before the next.

In terms of shape, round tables are useful because they can accommodate an odd number of people more easily and less noticeably. I try very hard never to have five or seven guests—it's a terrible number. A round table also encourages conversation to flow around it. On the other hand, rectangular tables are more readily extended and reduced to cope with varying numbers of guests, and if narrow, can be talked across which makes for a more interesting "mix" in the conversation.

MAKING MORE OF A TABLE

To entertain a larger number of guests, or to give myself more room for a generous centerpiece, I extend my table using a false table top, which I store in my pantry. The table top is simply a piece of unpainted board covered with green felt baize that I place over my smaller table for an instant table extension. Remember that it should not extend more than about 8in (20cm) in any direction or the table will become unstable.

THE COMFORT FACTOR

There is nothing worse than your legs going numb from sitting on a hard seat, so make sure your dining chairs are comfortable and well upholstered—and if not, add a cushion. Chairs should be a good weight—sturdy but not too heavy to pull to the table or push back. A chair should also be the correct height in relation to the table, so that the person sitting on it can easily reach the table.

Spacing and Placing

When arranging a table, make sure there is adequate room around it for people to come easily to their seats and to leave them. If you'll have staff serving, remember to allow sufficient space for them to pass behind each occupied chair. Traditionally, the host and hostess take their places at the head and foot of the table, with guests along the sides, but I prefer to sit in the middle of my guests, so that I can help conversation along and keep an eye on the removal and replenishment of plates and glasses. It's fun to place people beside someone they like or know, although they should be courteous enough to invite others to join in their conversation rather than just gossiping among themselves. Adventurous hosts often place people who don't know each other, but who have common interests or have traveled to similar places, side by side.

MIXING YOUR FRIENDS

If you are concerned about your mixture of guests or those who don't know each other, make the table a little smaller than normal and set places closer together. It is an essential part of a good host's job to introduce people who come alone or do not know other guests. You should be well briefed as to who guests are and what they do, so that when you make an introduction you can begin by giving a point of interest or something that the people being introduced will have in common, therefore giving them a subject on which to strike up conversation. You could also make the cocktails a little stronger and voilà, success will be yours.

TABLE SETTINGS

TABLE SETTINGS

In this section of the book, you will find masses of useful information on the elements that come together to create a beautiful table setting—you could call them my "tools of the trade." From choosing the right china and glassware, to selecting the perfect tablecloth and napkin, these are the ingredients to set the scene.

Selecting China

I have enough plates to serve dinner to 100 without borrowing anything, but then I have to confess to being something of a collector. I have eight main services of china that I use regularly, with other, smaller sets that I use from time to time.

The starting point is to have a good basic *mise en place*—a set of plates and bowls in a single color that you can use constantly and that allows you to create different looks with flowers, napkins, and detail. This style of china may be unadorned white or cream, but it doesn't have to be dull—it could have an impressed edge, such as a rim of raised rings or a subtle scallop.

Versatility is the key to a basic range. Look for a bowl with the shape and depth that you can use to serve breakfast cereal, soup, salad, pasta, and dessert. A standard dinner plate is 10–11in (25–27cm), a dessert plate is 8in (20cm), and a side plate is 6in (15cm), and you can serve any combination of courses on these. A 13in (33cm) charger makes a superb alternative to a place mat and, if chosen in a contrasting color to the main plate, adds a decorative element. Chargers and larger plates, however, may not fit into the dishwasher and will have to be washed by hand.

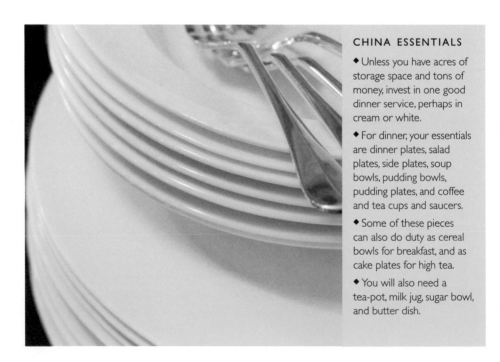

CHINA ESSENTIALS

◆ Unless you have acres of storage space and tons of money, invest in one good dinner service, perhaps in cream or white.

◆ For dinner, your essentials are dinner plates, salad plates, side plates, soup bowls, pudding bowls, pudding plates, and coffee and tea cups and saucers.

◆ Some of these pieces can also do duty as cereal bowls for breakfast, and as cake plates for high tea.

◆ You will also need a tea-pot, milk jug, sugar bowl, and butter dish.

To dress up your basic range, add several smaller sets of decorative dishes and plates—you'll need just enough to serve all your guests on the same plate for one course.

Chic tableware is usually fine English bone china or French porcelain, and these materials are most often used in formal dinner services. Most houses will also have an everyday range of basic household pottery that can be put in a microwave or dishwasher.

I also have handmade studio plates, which are perfect for a simple lunch or supper of home-made bread and delicious cheeses—stoneware and earthenware are appropriately rustic for this type of food. Other staples in my cupboard are glass and crystal plates, which can be used beside or on top of any type of china. Their lightness and transparency help give an appearance of space on the table. They are also colorless so go with anything I may choose.

I also like to use dishes or plates associated with the country or culture that has inspired the menu—for example, hand-thrown terracotta plates for an Italian feast or small porcelain bowls, chopsticks, and ceramic spoons for an Oriental dinner.

I am completely in favor of mixing different wares, as long as everyone is served the course on the same plate. For example, you could bring soup to the table in a colored bowl, and follow by serving the main course on a white plate, with salad on a crystal or glass side plate; dessert could be on a decorated fruit plate or in a stemmed glass. It's perfectly acceptable to mix gold- and silver-rimmed tableware. (Remember that gilded pieces should be washed by hand unless specifically designed to withstand the temperature and chemicals of a dishwasher.)

Choosing Crystal and Glassware

The basic crystal requirement is a set of water glasses, a set of red wine glasses and smaller glasses for white wine, a set of champagne flutes and two good water jugs or pitchers. Decanters, port glasses, sherry glasses, brandy glasses, and cocktail glasses may be added according to your tastes.

Matching glassware can look dull, so I like to mix not only patterns and styles but also colors and finishes. As with mixing china, make sure that all guests have the same glass for the same drink, although the decoration may vary.

Wine glasses should be stemmed or footed; use a large bowl for red wine, a smaller one for white. For casual meals I use a tumbler or double old-fashioned glass for water, and for formal occasions a large, colored stemmed glass. I use colored glassware only for water.

Don't be too concerned about "proper" use of glassware. If you have fabulous crystal champagne glasses, use them to serve a crisp chilled white wine, or for a casual supper of pasta and salad, a small and simple tumbler can be used for a robust red wine.

Glassware can also multitask. Sherry, liqueur, and brandy glasses and champagne flutes can all double as flower vases and stemmed glassware, such as champagne bowls, can be used to serve individual desserts such as fruit compote or mousse.

PLACING GLASSES

When setting the table, the water glass should be placed on the right of the place setting, above the knife. The other glasses should be placed in a row to the left of the water glass in order of use: white wine for the first course, red for the second course, and so on. If the row is too long, make a triangle.

WASHING GLASS AND CRYSTAL

When it comes to washing glass and crystal, I don't think any of the modern washing and rinsing products can beat the traditional bowl of warm soapy water. Wash crystal glasses one at a time and rinse them in clean tepid water. Be careful not to knock the glasses against taps or faucets. Leave the glasses to drain but not dry, then polish them with a lint-free cloth or linen glass towel. If you leave glasses to dry on a draining board, they often become marked by water drips so set them on a lint-free towel.

Choosing Cutlery and Silverware

It's well worth investing in good cutlery or flatware. The basic canteen of domestic cutlery will have six to twelve table knives, table forks, dessert/cheese knives, dessert forks, dessert spoons, soup spoons, and teaspoons, with a pair of serving spoons. Traditional canteens also used to have fish knives and forks as well as fruit knives and forks, but these are not often used in modern households. More recent additions to the canteen are steak knives and forks, the knife having a serrated edge that makes it more suitable for cutting thick meat. Where a soup spoon is not available, a serving spoon can be substituted, which I much prefer.

Decorative spoons, such as those with colorful enamel insets or handles embedded with semiprecious stones, are often set aside for coffee but they can also be used for sorbet or delicate desserts. I also like to have a set of knives and forks slightly smaller than those for the main course, to use for salads and hors d'oeuvres. I often use antique fruit knives and forks for a cheese course.

SHOPPING FOR CUTLERY

Even if you look rather odd, it's a good idea to pretend to eat with it before you buy it. There's nothing worse than a knife-handle which is too thin to be held comfortably in the hand.

SETTING THE TABLE

Place cutlery so that you work from the outside in: the smaller knives and forks for the first course on the outside and the larger for the main course next to the plate. The soup spoon should go on the right with the knives. Line them up so that the bottom of the handles are in a straight line. Pudding spoons and forks can be placed above the plate or at the inside nearest the center of the setting down the sides—it's a matter of personal choice. A butter knife is set on the side plate. Once you have finished eating, the knife and fork should be placed together with the handles toward you and prongs upward. However, in the United States, they should be placed diagonally across your plate with the handles at 4 o'clock.

CRUETS

Traditionally, cruets were small stoppered bottles that contained condiments, but now the term embraces containers that hold salt, pepper, mustard, and accompaniments such as soya or wasabi. Coarse salt is usually presented in a small open dish with a spoon, whereas fine salt can be shaken from a cellar. The same

applies to pepper, although for coarse-ground pepper a mill is usually offered. For formal occasions, small ceramic dishes, glass bowls, or silver cellars are more appropriate.

Candlelight

A well-dressed table is the star of the show and should always be the focus of attention as you enter the room. In the evening, this is easily achieved by dimming the ambient electric lighting so that the majority of the room is in shadow, and drawing attention to the table with an appropriate number of candles. If the room is decorated in a different color to those used on the table, casting soft shadows in this way makes this less noticeable. Candlelight is undeniably flattering to all skin tones and will also reflect off polished silver and crystal, making it glow and sparkle.

CANDLESTICKS

Candlesticks and candelabra do bring elegance to a table and are the traditional method of distributing light, but now we have other choices.

HURRICANE SHADES

A hurricane shade can be filled with so many things. Here (below) I surrounded the base of the candles with rose petals, but you could use pebbles and shells, nuts, or crystal chandelier drops, or try coiling handfuls of green rushes or other long, pliable stems around the base.

VOTIVES OR TEA LIGHTS

Bring candlelight down to the level of the table is an essential "trick" to improving the view. I now often only use tea lights or votives placed in attractive containers, such as those made of tin, ceramic, crystal, silver, mercury glass, or whatever medium takes my fancy.

Tablecloths

The tablecloth is the foundation of a setting. Center it so the creases run straight down the table. After use, deal immediately with any stains and iron carefully before folding and putting away so that the creases are neat. (If you have closet space, hang your tablecloths like trousers on a wooden coathanger after ironing, to avoid unnecessary creasing.) It is worth investing in good heavy cotton or linen in white as it can be bleached or boiled to remove heavy staining. For a polished formal dining table, one should invest in a heat-resistant material cut to fit the table, so that any cloth can then be placed over the top without fear of damaging the table surface. This should be stored in the pantry.

Cotton is widely used for table linens and can be plain or woven with a self-pattern, such as jacquard, where the design appears within the material. Colors can also be woven in or printed onto cotton. As long as the design is colorfast, it can be washed at a high temperature, and can be starched for a crisp appearance. Linen is generally heavier than cotton and has a longer life expectancy—some of my linen cloths and napkins date from the 1900s. Linen can be very finely woven, as in fine Irish linen, or more coarsely woven, resulting in slub and texture on the surface. Fine linen is ideal for formal entertaining, while the coarser finish is attractive for casual occasions. I love to bring the unexpected to table settings and sometimes use a fine wool plaid blanket or a crocheted bed cover instead of a cloth. Equally fun can be seersucker fabric or a vintage shawl.

For a formal evening, use a floor-length undercloth that reflects your color theme and add a white cloth on top. The top cloth should be smaller, so that the undercloth can be seen. As a rule of thumb, the diameter of a circular cloth (or the width and length of a rectangular one) should be about 12in (30cm) more than the table, so the topper has a drop of about 6in (15cm).

Napkins

Napkins should be folded into a neat rectangle, or rolled and placed in a napkin ring or tied attractively. If you place the napkin on the plate, it makes it quite clear whose is whose and adds to the decoration of the setting. If the first course is already on the table, place the napkin on the left of the forks.

Unfold your napkin once seated and place it on your lap. At the end of the meal, don't refold it but leave it by your place setting or on your chair.

It is amusing to think "outside the box" and to use wonderful old linen tea towels or large polka-dot handkerchiefs in place of regular napkins. There are many classic ways of folding napkins, too: the water lily, the slipper, and the fan are just a few of the styles that would have appeared on well-dressed Victorian tables. But I like a napkin to look as though it is ready for use, so I generally choose simple rolls or folds. A napkin can be an ideal place to make a personal welcome to a guest, by writing their name on a luggage tag and tying it on, or even by embroidering it with their name. Try using simple garden twine with luggage labels or white flower buds with sophisticated silver rings, beaded bracelets, or hair-tie pom-poms. I find that napkin rings provide a great opportunity to introduce a little humor to the table.

STICKY FINGERS

When serving seafood, artichokes, or anything that involves using the hands to shell, peel, or dissect food, I set two table napkins at each place setting. The first napkin is to tuck in at the neck to protect the shirt or blouse from drips and spills, while the second is for the lap and hands.

A small crystal finger bowl filled with tepid water, decorated with a pretty flower petal or a strip of citrus zest, is also useful. Allow one bowl for each diner.

Flowers

The main rule for arranging flowers for a table is that the display should be either above or below the eye level of people conversing across the table. The guests should be able to have direct eye contact with the person they are talking to without having to duck around the flowers. When you are using glass or crystal vases, remember that it isn't just the flower heads that are on show—you'll see the stems as well, so they should be clean, neatly cut, and placed in clear water.

I always try to find flowers that are in season. Forced flowers don't last, and one of the nice things about holding a party at home is that you can have the pleasure and enjoyment of the flowers during the following days.

I put flowers on the table at the last moment, partly because the room will be warm and could cause the flowers to open or droop and partly to keep the cloth or table surface as pristine as possible. Individual buds on napkins need to be positioned just before the guests come to the table because the buds have to survive without water.

For a special party, I like to put individual flower heads at each place setting—you could use a head of the flowers in the main arrangement. Equally, if you can only find

CHOOSING VASES

I recommend acquiring a basic "wardrobe" of three or four bud vases to hold individual stems, a tall flute vase for a few elegant sprays, and a low vase or deep dish that can be used for a centerpiece (centerpieces should be kept below 8in/20cm in height). Make sure the container does not clash with your chosen blooms; glass and crystal are safe choices, as they suit every type of flower. For special parties, an individual flower can decorate each place setting—use tiny crystal shot glasses as vases.

a few jaded blooms, don't despair—put the best heads in small individual bowls or pull off the petals and use them around the base of candles or scattered over the cloth.

I often use flowers to bring out the color of the tablecloth or napkins, but avoid very strongly scented flowers, as they'll compete with the food and overwhelm your taste buds. I use highly scented flowers only in the entry hall and sitting room (the same rule applies to using scented candles).

If I am entertaining in town I sometimes choose a single flower, such as a white rose, and fill a large champagne cooler with dozens of them. In the country I mix the blooms and have a less formal arrangement—it's about encompassing the ambience of the setting and style of entertaining.

When choosing flowers for a table center or arrangement it is advisable to select a limited range of colors—two at most plus foliage, and for a smart dinner even a single color can be sufficient. Be sparing with the blooms and avoid cramming too many into

a container—each flower head should have space so that it can be seen and admired, and although trailing fronds may look romantic, make sure that they don't interfere with the placements or food. Although silver and ceramic vases are attractive in certain settings, cut crystal and glass will sit comfortably on any table and with any type of flower.

Good-looking fruit and vegetables also make an informal centerpiece. I like to cut a few pieces of fruit open—but choose fruit that won't go brown or dribble, such as pomegranates or lemons. Foliage and grasses can also be arranged to make a stunning centerpiece or used to bind a napkin.

Place Cards

For formal dinners, or gatherings of large numbers of people, place cards are an essential part of the table setting—my own range of place cards (see page 138) is ideal. People always like to know where you would like them to sit, and a table plan ensures that like-minded people can be placed together, or kindly souls seated next to nervous guests.

For informal lunches and suppers, have fun with the place cards and try something unusual. For instance, a small paper luggage label tied around a monogramed napkin with string makes a perfect place card. The rough string complements the place mat, and both are set against the smooth napkin and glazed plate. If you are handy with a needle and thread, you could embroider your guests' names onto plain napkins, or search out initialed items, such as key fobs, which guests can then take home with them.

SPECIAL
OCCASIONS

SPECIAL OCCASIONS

I love to design tables for special occasions—birthdays, anniversaries, Christmas and Easter, and any excuse I can think of to throw a party or host a dinner. In this section, you will find photographs and ideas for themed table settings for every occasion, whether you are hosting a formal dinner for 20 people or planning an intimate supper for two, designing a theme for a children's birthday tea or putting together a casual weekday supper.

Informal Summer Lunch

This table is in a glorious setting, next to the pool at a friend's home in the Spanish mountains. This is outdoor living at its most delicious.

For this relaxed summer lunch table, I have chosen blue-and-white textiles—vintage linens, faded denims, and striped cottons—to introduce a touch of masculine glamour. I have kept each setting within the confines of the place mat to maintain that sense of order. Great earthenware pots of viburnum and feathery fennel and lemons picked from the tree in the garden stand on an ancient stone sink, contrasting with the formality of the place settings.

The first course of locally grown artichokes is already on the table. In this atmosphere, I like to have the first course placed on the table before guests are seated. The authority of the cook is dispensed with, drinks can be finished at leisure, and there is no need to hurry. My choice of glasses, plates, and table linen reflects this uncluttered haven: stripes, checks, little ornamentation. The many textures play off each other in a harmony of blue and white. All is clean, pure, and beautiful.

Informal Winter Lunch

To me, this is an honest table with earthiness and purity, yet it encompasses a spectrum of natural shades—the deep glaze of the candlesticks and plant pots, the honey wood, the biscuit place mats, the creamy pottery, and napkins. Each and every detail of the setting is beautiful, like a still-life painting. The textures are a balance of coarse and smooth—the polished wooden table and smooth glazed pottery juxtaposed with the rough linen mats. Wine and water are served in stoneware jugs and bottles; the candlesticks complement the hand-thrown earthenware plates. Ornate cut-crystal glasses would look out of place on this table, so I have used rustic hand-blown glasses, each one a little different from the next but in keeping with the handmade pottery. Instead of using cut flowers I used early-flowering spring bulbs.

This simple rustic setting reminds me of being in Provence, eating French cheeses and freshly baked baguettes, washed down with a glass of good locally produced wine. Even when I come home, I find it therapeutic and relaxing to re-create a meal that captures that feeling of carefree enjoyment.

Summer Supper

This simple but charming table setting is ideal for a casual supper with friends or close family. It is pretty, stylish, and perfect for entertaining any age group. All that's needed are a few basic but carefully chosen elements to put the look together. White china, elegant crystal, and old linen napkins are placed around antique pewter chargers, whose worn surfaces complement the well-used tabletop with its rich patina and act as a foil to the pristine white linen and china. The folded napkins form a background for the cutlery, and delicate flower buds are used to highlight the fine embroidery on the fabric surface.

By keeping the setting uncomplicated and monotone, the food that is brought to the table becomes the focus of attention—its color, texture, and aroma will be the key features. I like to leave simple food and fine ingredients to bask in their own glory—a plain glass bowl or dish or a neutral colored plate is all that is required. On occasions such as this I am especially careful when selecting my ingredients at the market.

This simple white table setting also makes a good base or starting point for creating a scheme with touches of color. You can follow this basic style but then add a signature or feature color, such as pink napkins and rosebuds, or green chargers and napkins tied with fronds of lemongrass, giving just a subtle hint of color.

Winter Supper

I love spending the weekend pottering in the kitchen and dreaming up warming receipts at this time of year, so Friday night supper is always a good but simple table—with no fuss but lots of style, naturally. This table is really all about making my friends feel that I've made an effort for them but without making them feel intimidated.

Traveling as I do subjects me to endless different and varied situations, so I was gripped when visiting a friend of mine in New England, who, preparing supper for family and local chums, threw a tartan blanket on her table with the exclamation, "Honey, I hate ironing! And surely the point of a great table is change." Its subtle heathery colors dictated the palette of cream, purple, and deep blue. So, with the addition of a set of sparkling indigo-blue glasses and salt cellars, horn-handled cutlery, and some earthy studio pottery, the table setting is completed in minutes. Focus on layering up color, texture, and contrast, with a touch of novelty, then just add a bottle of good wine for simple style.

The Perfect Breakfast

These days it is rare to get time to enjoy a leisurely breakfast so when the opportunity does arise we should make the most of it. First of all, think of ease and comfort—well-upholstered chairs, plenty of room to spread out the newspapers, good light to read by, and a radio in the background so that conversation is not essential (I am toxic before 10am!).

I usually set the breakfast table the night before, so that it requires no effort in the morning. I squeeze grapefruits and oranges and place the juice in my glass bottles in the refrigerator to chill overnight. The setting is simple but the few pieces used are of good quality, such as crisp linen napkins and hand-decorated studio stoneware plates. I use dinner plates because each is big enough to serve as a tray, a plate, and a saucer, so you aren't left with dreary piles of washing-up.

Simple touches, such as wrapping the warm bread in a nineteenth-century French napkin before laying it in a shallow basket and decanting local honey, home-made jam, and butter into glass or ceramic pots, make all the difference. Don't forget to provide a butter knife and a spoon for each jam or honey.

Add a bowl of ripe fruit as an edible table decoration. Fruit and flowers can be used to denote the season. A winter breakfast, for example, might feature a pot of Christmas roses and a bowl of tangerines; in the fall, a basket of crisp red apples and blackberries with a vase of late-flowering roses; and for summer, a dish of freshly picked raspberries and strawberries with a few sweet peas in a glass.

The thing I love most about breakfast is that the smell of warm bread and good coffee drifts through the house and under bedroom doors, except when I burn the toast, so even the late risers will find it difficult to linger under the sheets for long.

Breakfast in Bed

Sometimes a friend will arrive unexpectedly or at short notice and stay for a night; thankfully my guest rooms are always prepared. The following morning, to make them feel especially welcome and to start their day on a good note, I like to present my guests with an uncomplicated wake-up tray.

The modern zinc tray that I usually use is large enough to rest safely on your lap in bed—I find a small, unstable tray and crumbly food a nuisance in bed, but a good-sized tray or one with legs that will fit comfortably over your legs makes the whole experience more enjoyable and indulgent. If providing tea, coffee, or hot chocolate, use a heat-absorbent mat and remember not to over-fill the cup.

I cover the surface of the tray with a crisp square of linen—the cloth doesn't have to be the same size and shape as the tray because it is more to do with the quality and appearance than the fit. As I have drawers packed full of favorite small linen cloths and single napkins, I love having the opportunity to select a couple of special pieces and put them on show. An unpretentious glass filled with a few fresh flowers from the garden and a pretty plate with a gilded edge are all that's needed to turn the start of an average day into something quite special.

Afternoon Tea

The institution of having tea hasn't changed much since my childhood and I like to capture that feeling of nostalgia and times gone by with traditional blue-and-white Spode china and plenty of home-made jams and cakes. I have drawers full of pieces of vintage linen such as small cloths, mats, and unmatched napkins, and they come into their own when friends come over for tea and a cake. Tea is a pleasant, calming institution that is easy to prepare.

The skill is to keep it relaxed and to make it appear as though tea has arrived effortlessly! The setting is therefore undemanding and based on a layering of pattern on pattern. I started with the vintage blue-and-white checked cotton cloth, laid with the patterned china, a Georgian silver teapot and milk jug, and a little pot of spring flowers. To finish, I added embroidered napkins pulled through a child's elasticated bracelet, which makes a perfect, jolly napkin ring.

I like to decant honey and jam into pots. This makes them look so much more appealing than serving them in screw-top jars with a sticky label across the front. I love making my own jam so this gives me a perfect opportunity to use my visitors as guinea pigs!

THE PERFECT CUP OF TEA

One good teaspoon of leaves is sufficient to make two cups of tea. The pot should be pre-warmed with a little hot water, which is then thrown away. The tea leaves are placed in the pot, and the hot water poured over them and left to brew for three to four minutes before pouring. Always make sure that you have a tea-leaf strainer and small bowl handy.

Dining by Candlelight

Any room lit entirely by candlelight has a magical theatrical feel. But to dine in this room—in which every plane is lavishly decorated and adorned, every inch of the deep cornice is distressed and gilded, and every surface glows in the flickering candlelight—is to experience a feeling of total opulence.

The colors of topaz, amethyst, tourmaline, and gold are used to full effect in this palace of flickering light. For this formal dinner, I selected plain white linen mats, which allow the wonderful figuring and grain of the wooden table to be seen. This rich surface frames and highlights the polished crystal and shining silver, which can sometimes become secondary in an elaborate array of cloth, napkins, and embellishment.

Traditional Formality

This formal dinner has a very traditional setting. From the golden twinkling of the chandelier to the perfectly smooth white damask tablecloth, the atmosphere speaks of quality, permanence, and, above all, a great pride in tradition.

I encapsulated that sense of timelessness with copious quantities of candles. The table is lit almost entirely by candlelight and its gentle flicker can be seen from the wall sconces and the hurricane shades. I looked for pieces that would gleam, shimmer, and reflect the flickering golden light of the many candles. Down the center of the table I placed a long, oval Charles X *place-surtout* made of mirror with ormolu gallery mounts. As dusk falls, the mirrored surface will reflect and amplify the candlelight.

The hostess owns an incredible and venerable Sevres porcelain dinner service. Inspired by the classical architecture of the room and the yellow of the porcelain, I created a table setting that was rich in embellishment and style. I chose amethyst and an off-white coffee-flecked damask as a backdrop. The table is arranged in a classic format, with the centerpiece being the tallest item on the table and the most eye-catching.

Valentine's Day Surprise

This simple, measured setting is perfect for a Valentine supper—it isn't necessary to cover everything with red to get the message across. Here, the white roses and tall stems of tuberoses are enough to convey a heartfelt message. You could also use a setting like this for an engagement dinner, as a way of saying in a very private setting what you have been trying to say for months!

The muted and natural earthy shades of the tabletop and tableware are brought to life here with the vivid splashes of pure white napkins and flowers, finished with hints of fresh green. I have also introduced a few pieces of unusual cutlery, such as the spoon made from polished coconut shell, to give a more rustic look against the decorated crystal.

CREATING AN INTIMATE SETTING

An intimate lunch or supper for just two is easy to transport to a new and less predictable setting, so take a table and a couple of chairs to another part of your home for a different view on life. On a sunny spring day you could position them by a window overlooking the garden or in the winter by a roaring fire in a study or sitting room. Use your imagination to move beyond the conventional setting of the dining room or kitchen. A major part of the art of entertaining is creating the element of surprise.

Mother's Day Lunch

Without question, the most important people in anyone's life are one's parents, and to pay special tribute to an adored mother is particularly satisfying. Whether it be on a birthday, on Mother's Day, or just to say thank you, it is worth taking a little extra time to make it a memorable event and in some small way to show appreciation for the years of comfort, advice, and love that she has shared with you.

This gorgeous table was designed for a special lunch a friend was having with her sisters in honor of their mother. To oblige, I brought together a festival of rose pink and sparkling crystal to give the occasion a magical touch that also suited the recipients.

Scented roses, full-blown peonies, and night-scented stocks subtly fill the air with the sweetest of fragrances. An antique embroidered Indian organdie shawl is added as a delicate overcloth, with a generous scattering of pink rose petals, and pretty beaded bracelets are used as napkin rings. A furl of pink ribbon augments the beauty of a tazza of freshly baked macaroons in pastel colors—lifting the food above the table with a tazza or a piece of stemmed glassware creates such a glamorous effect. The place settings are close together on this compact round table to bring intimacy to this wonderfully private moment.

Birthday Tea

Tea is so well suited to our older relatives—
it agrees with their metabolism! I set up
this tea table in the drawing room for
the birthday of a friend's grandmother.
This gave the celebration intimacy and
comfort, which, in my experience, is what
grandmothers like. I set a scene of old-
fashioned prettiness and ease, using an ivory
silk quilted counterpane as a tablecloth,
liberally and traditionally decorated with
pale pink roses arranged singly and in pairs
in small glass vases.

I chose well-upholstered chairs with arms because I suspected this celebratory
tea could cheerfully turn to cocktails as the evening drew in. Champagne corks would
be popped and all the girls would have a lively, giggly time and would need to be
comfortably settled in. So that there should be no awkwardness among the guests as

to whether cocktails were a possibility or
not, I boldly set out prettily engraved
champagne saucers at each place so that
later tea and cakes turned to something
a little more festive.

On this occasion, a candelabra made a
wonderful centerpiece encircled by silver
candlesticks, so that the flickering light
came from many heights.

The prettiest, whitest starched napkins
were absolutely essential here—the
scalloped edges and delicate embroidery
are perfection. I love to make guests feel
special, so placed a little boxed gift of soap
at each place.

Children's Birthday Tea

Needlework was the inspiration behind the fun setting created for this children's tea party. It all started with the colorful crocheted bed cover that I grew up with, which I laid over a well-scrubbed kitchen table. Picking up on the vintage feel of the cloth, I added 1950s napkins and embellished them with pom-pom hair ties, which the girls took home as presents at the end. Although some people regard table napkins as old-fashioned, I think they are an essential part of any table—even for young children. Jammy fingers and chocolate-smeared lips can be easily wiped clean if each child has their own napkin.

The colorful theme of the tablecloth was carried through with sticky buns sprinkled lavishly with multicolored hundreds and thousands and chocolate cake dotted with sweet decorations. My approach when catering for a children's party is to give them the kind of food they enjoy and understand—it won't upset their nutritional balance to have custard tarts, chocolate cake, cookies, and biscuits once in a while. As all the food can be eaten with fingers, the plates and cups are kept to a minimum, leaving more room for the fun things—toys and cakes.

Not all of the food on the table is real, however—some of the cakes and tarts are knitted. This joke food interspersed amongst the copious quantity of delicious edible treats drew peals of laughter from both the children and their parents and made the whole party an unforgettable event, with many of the parents remarking that it was reminiscent of their own childhood.

A Contemporary Christmas

As so much of Christmas is focused on the younger members of the family, I like to hold a Christmas Eve dinner just for the grown-ups. When the children have gone to bed and the house is quiet, I begin my favorite Christmas ritual: setting the table with the most beautiful and beloved pieces from my china cupboard. Never be scared of opulence—I am a firm believer that quality never dates.

For this dinner, I found gold in nineteenth-century embossed gilt cutlery, a pair of laurel-leaf candelabra, and shimmering gold-rimmed wine glasses. Specially commissioned, handmade crackers filled with gifts are covered with crinkled paper reminiscent of fabulous Fortuny evening gowns. Finally, I have gold almond dragées cascading from cranberry glass chests with ormolu mounts; these add more than a touch of decadence and opulence to a glittering *mise en place*.

A Country Christmas

With my entire family gathering for Christmas at our house, I created a fabulously festive table that diffused warmth, affection, wonder, and amusement for the perfect feast. It was an occasion to use my most special things, and to add a few surprises. I combined old and new, simple and costly, to enchant all my family. I gave free rein to caprice, setting a flock of knitted sheep to wander among the vintage crystal and bridge the seventy-year age difference between the youngest and oldest seated at the table. In such a setting, everyone relaxes quickly and a vital atmosphere was created.

At Christmas I always make a special effort to decorate the drawing room and hall as well as the dining room. I usually take one color and use it liberally throughout my Christmas theme. Here it is ruby red.

The flickering light of candles illuminates the room, playing on the old facet-cut crystal that I love to bring out at Christmas. Tinsel and glitter has its place but not here.

Red roses and berries punctuate the strong evergreens, while the flagons of claret have a gorgeous dark intensity against the white tablecloths and napkins.

The traditions of Christmas are all here and I make them beautiful and suitable to my needs. The excellent whole Stilton (God forbid the multiple choice of the cheeseboard!) is swathed in a white napkin and decorated with a sprig of sage. The wine and port are served in fine old crystal, and mince pies are offered on a cake-stand.

Easter Lunch

Easter is a time of celebration and hope, marking the end of winter and the beginning of spring. Among the great joys of this time is the abundance of flowers, such as daffodils, narcissi, hyacinths, and tulips, which can be gathered by the armful, and the promise of longer days lifts the spirits. I dressed this table with a dear friend, who was having a family Easter lunch. As the guests ranged in age from her grandmother to a young niece, we decided to add a dash of humor and an element of surprise with amusing napkins rings, hidden chocolate eggs, and tiny toys to give to the children while the grown-ups chatted over lunch. I used nineteenth-century Mason's Ironstone plates with copious quantities of well-polished family silver and crystal. The tall flutes above the table are stuffed with beautiful spring flowers.

Thanksgiving Night

Wrap up warm, kick up your heels, and enjoy yourself is the moral of this story. Thanksgiving is being celebrated in upstate Vermont. It's November, the night is clear, cold, and starry, but in a nineteenth-century hay barn, lit only by candles, fiddlers are playing, feet are stamping, and a barn dance is in full swing.

This traditional Thanksgiving supper takes the form of a generous picnic with organic wild turkey served in raffia boxes, buffet-style. The small, medium, and large picnic baskets, lined with old-fashioned greaseproof paper, admirably denote the three courses. The guests will settle down to eat with whom they like and where they like. The colors of the decorations are autumnal and suggested by the natural hues of the interior of the barn—straw, oak, and the olive-green painted benches. Abundant fruit and vegetables decorate the trestle tables—this is Thanksgiving, after all.

I love exploring the relationship between food and flowers. Decorations of gorgeously fresh vegetables are perfect for a festival such as Thanksgiving. I dispensed with flowers altogether and heaped creamy florets of cauliflower in a shining bowl, and arranged acid-green grapes in high vases with heads of broccoli. I nestled squat church candles in glass dishes of crimson-veined Swiss chard and purple and green asparagus. Strawberries glowed scarlet in the candlelight in small baskets. Freshly baked rustic loaves were piled high.

A Wedding Breakfast

This wedding was held at home, using garden flowers and family possessions handed down through generations, giving an intensely personal atmosphere to the proceedings. The wedding breakfast was laid out in this clapboard garden room, and the solemnity of the ceremony gave way to feasting and much hilarity.

On a personal occasion such as a wedding, don't let yourself be bullied by erroneous ideas of coordination. Use treasured and beautiful things where you can. I loathe seeing the wedding breakfast decked out in hired glasses, plates, and flatware just for the sake of uniformity, like a conference dinner in a business hotel. Use flowers and color to give coherence to your theme. I adored the rich green of a length of antique silk velvet and threw it over the top table. As I added to the table, pinks, golds, and greengage shades of green were soon singing against the sumptuous fabric, the gold detail of the eighteenth-century plates, the shining crystal and family silver, the pink rose petals, delicate blossom, and the fresh green mopheads of the hydrangeas. I also dyed intricately embroidered linen napkins a soft greengage for the occasion—it's fun to do something that's unique and special.

There is an intense beauty in the juxtaposition of the elements on the serving table. Strings of pearls tumble into cherry blossom. Meringues are cradled in crystal comports and adorned with petals. Rich red strawberries glow through crystal, and black-purple grapes cascade. The beauty of the food is essential: the deep pinks, reds, and purples of the fruit, the rich depth of the chocolate, and the ephemeral lightness of the meringues. Wedding food must work with the ambience. It must be simple, beautiful, and classy. Above all, it must be informally enjoyed.

I strove to infuse this display with passion. The possibilities for effusive decoration are boundless. Forget restricting convention—a wedding is an opportunity when everything may still not be enough.

Cocktail Hour

It is hugely enjoyable to invite a group of friends home for cocktails before going to the theater, or even after a concert or dinner at a restaurant. Make the occasion special by preparing a tray beforehand with a starched white linen cloth, a generous vase of flowers, and an array of beautifully polished glasses—I love to have a collection of assorted glasses ready so that I can serve whatever drink takes a guest's fancy.

Here a basket-weave crystal wine cooler makes a fine container for a generous bouquet of white and cream flowers, and matches the tall tumblers and decanter. A decanter of malt whiskey, cognac, or a fortified wine such as port or sherry is an inviting sight on a well-arranged tray. If appropriate, a few hors d'oeuvres are always a welcome accompaniment.

Drinks before Supper

Cocktail hour in hot countries is heaven: a shower and fresh clothes with the warmth of the sun still glowing on your skin, the expectation of a delicious supper, and an ice-cold cocktail to relax with by the pool. Here shades of blue against the natural yellows of stone and wood create a perfectly tranquil scene—a place to relax as an ice-cold drink is gently placed in your hand.

Keep a selection of glasses to hand. Make sure beers are in the refrigerator and there's plenty of ice. Don't go overboard with salty snacks. To my mind, a few bitter black olives and salted nuts are perfection. A handful of flowering sage plucked from the garden on the way to the poolhouse adds a simple yet charming touch.

RECIPES FOR ENTERTAINING

Appetizers
Entrées
Accompaniments
Desserts
Cocktails
Pairing Food and Wine

RECIPES FOR ENTERTAINING

Here is a small selection of some of my favorite recipes.
These are fail-safe dishes: some can be prepared in advance, and
all are sure to impress your guests. At the end of this section, you
will find recipes for cocktails—a sure-fire way to ensure your
guests enjoy their evening.

· APPETIZERS ·

Roasted eggplant and prosciutto salad

Prosciutto makes the best crispy bacon any kitchen can produce, so
start cooking and impress with your guests.

SERVES 4

8 oz (200 g) 1½ cups
  cherry tomatoes

2 small eggplants/aubergines,
  sliced lengthwise

2 tablespoons olive oil

4 slices prosciutto

a bunch of arugula/rocket

salt and freshly ground black
  pepper

DRESSING

1 tablespoon balsamic
  vinegar

1 tablespoon Dijon mustard

3 tablespoons extra virgin
  olive oil

salt and freshly ground black
  pepper

Preheat the oven to 180°C (350°F) Gas 4.

Slice off and discard the top of each tomato, then put
them, cut side up, into an oiled roasting pan. Add the
eggplant/aubergines. Sprinkle with the olive oil, salt, and
pepper. Cook in the preheated oven for 15 minutes, then
reduce to 150°C (300°F) Gas 2 and cook for a further
15 minutes, until the tomatoes have burst their skins. Remove
from the oven and set aside. Cook the prosciutto under a hot
broiler/grill for about 3 minutes on each side, until crisp.

To make the dressing, put the vinegar and mustard into
a small bowl and mix until smooth. Gradually add the oil,
mixing well, then add salt and pepper to taste. Arrange the
arugula/rocket and roasted eggplant and tomatoes on plates
and spoon over the dressing. Top with the prosciutto and serve
warm or at room temperature.

Smoked and fresh salmon terrine

A mousseline is a mousse of fish, shellfish, or poultry lightened with cream and egg whites. When made with salmon, it is the most beautiful, elegant, golden-pink. It is amazingly easy to prepare too, with a spectacular effect that makes a very luxurious appetizer or posh picnic dish.

SERVES 6

8 oz (250 g) skinless salmon fillet, cut into chunks

1 teaspoon finely grated unwaxed orange zest

2 teaspoons freshly squeezed orange juice

4 tablespoons chopped fresh dill or chervil

14 oz (400 g) smoked salmon

2 egg whites, chilled

5 fl oz (150 ml) ⅔ cup heavy/whipping cream, chilled

freshly ground white pepper

red salad leaves, to serve

Put the chunks of fresh salmon in a food processor with the orange zest, orange juice, dill or chervil, and plenty of pepper. Blend until smooth. Remove the bowl from the food processor, cover, and chill in the refrigerator.

Preheat the oven to 180°C (350°F) Gas 4. Prepare a 1½-pint (900-ml) 4-cup terrine mold by lightly oiling and base-lining with wax/greaseproof paper.

Roughly chop half the smoked salmon. Put the bowl back on the processor. With the machine running, add the egg whites through the feed tube, then the cream. Blend until thick and smooth—do not overwork or it will curdle. Scrape into a bowl, then stir in the chopped smoked salmon. Carefully fill the prepared terrine with the mixture, packing down well. Level the surface and cover the top with buttered wax paper. Stand the terrine in a roasting pan and pour in hot water to come halfway up the sides. Bake in the preheated oven for 35–40 minutes until firm. Remove from the oven, let cool completely, then chill in the refrigerator.

Loosen the edges of the terrine with a thin knife and turn out onto a wooden board. Trim and tidy up the edges and pat dry. Wrap the terrine with the remaining smoked salmon, pressing down well, then transfer to a flat serving platter. Slice the terrine with a very sharp knife and serve with red salad leaves.

· ENTRÉES ·

Chicken, lemon, and green olive tagine

A fabulously fragrant chicken casserole that can be easily made ahead
of time and reheated just before serving.

SERVES 6

12 skinless, boneless chicken
thighs, about 2¼ lbs (1 kg)
in total

3 tablespoons olive oil

2 onions (14 oz/400 g),
sliced

2 garlic cloves, crushed

a good pinch of saffron
threads

½ pint (300 ml) 1 cup chicken
or light vegetable stock

1 teaspoon finely grated fresh
ginger or ½ teaspoon
ground ginger

2 small preserved lemons

2½ oz (75 g) pitted green
olives marinated with herbs

a small bunch of fresh cilantro/
coriander with its stalks

1–2 tablespoons freshly
squeezed lemon juice

sea salt and freshly ground
black pepper

1 teaspoon harissa paste
(a hot and spicy Moroccan
chili paste), to serve
(optional)

Remove any excess fat from the chicken thighs and cut them in half. Heat the oil in a large cast-iron casserole or lidded skillet/frying pan, add the sliced onions and garlic, and cook over medium heat for 7–8 minutes until the onions have started to soften and collapse. Add the chicken thighs, mix well with the onions, and continue to cook for about 10 minutes over low heat, stirring occasionally.

Put the saffron in a mortar or small bowl and crush with a pestle. Pour over 2 tablespoons of the stock and leave for a few minutes to infuse. Stir the saffron and ginger into the chicken.

Quarter the preserved lemons, scoop out the flesh, and finely slice the peel. Halve the olives, then add the olives and preserved lemon to the chicken. Pour in the remaining stock and mix well. Thoroughly wash the cilantro/coriander, cut off the stalks, tie them together with a piece of cotton or string, and lay them in the casserole. Put a lid on the pan and leave to simmer until the chicken is cooked (about another 30 minutes).

Remove the cilantro stalks and season the tagine to taste with lemon juice, salt, and pepper. Put the harissa paste, if using, into a bowl, spoon off 4–5 tablespoons of the liquid from the tagine, and mix with the harissa. Roughly chop the cilantro leaves, stir into the tagine, and serve the harissa on the side for those that want it.

Roast fillet of beef with soy and butter sauce

The soy and butter sauce may sound unconventional, but it makes a very light, savory, meaty sauce that is much more wine friendly than some of the very intense, winey reductions you get in restaurants.

SERVES 6

1 teaspoon coarse sea salt

2 teaspoons black peppercorns

½ teaspoon ground allspice

1 tablespoon all-purpose/ plain flour

18–20 oz (1–1.1 kg) fillet of beef

1 tablespoon sunflower or light olive oil

3 tablespoons (40 g) soft butter

2 tablespoons Madeira or dry Marsala

¾ pint (375 ml) 1½ cups fresh beef stock or stock made with ¾ organic, low-salt beef bouillon/stock cube

1½ tablespoons Japanese soy sauce

Preheat the oven to 225°C (425°F) Gas 7.

Put the coarse salt and peppercorns in a mortar and grind with a pestle until finely ground. Mix in the allspice and flour. Remove any fat or sinew from the beef fillet and dry thoroughly with paper towels. Put the seasoning and flour on a plate and roll the beef in the mixture, patting it evenly into the surface and shaking off any excess.

Put a cast-iron casserole or deep roasting pan over medium to high heat, add the oil and half the butter, and brown the beef quickly on all sides. Transfer to the preheated oven and roast for 20–40 minutes, depending how thick your beef fillet is and how rare you like it. Remove from the oven and set aside for 10–15 minutes, lightly covered with foil. Pour off any excess fat in the pan, leaving about 1 tablespoon. Pour in the Madeira and let it bubble up for a few seconds, then add the stock and soy sauce. Bring to the boil, turn the heat down a little, and reduce by half. Pour any juices that have accumulated under the meat into the pan, whisk in the remaining butter, and season with black pepper (you shouldn't need any salt).

Carve the meat into thick slices and serve on warmed plates with the sauce spooned over and served with some roast new potatoes and green beans.

Lamb navarin

A fantastic dish that can be made in advance, then just finished off on the day:
this makes your life easier and also improves the flavor of the dish. Choose
vegetables to suit your taste: try leeks, cauliflower and broccoli florets, asparagus,
parsnips, turnips, pumpkin, or sweet potatoes—the list is endless.

SERVES 8

4 lbs (2 kg) boneless leg or
   shoulder of lamb, cubed

3 tablespoons olive oil

3 tablespoons all-purpose/
   plain flour

2 pints (1 litre) 4 cups
   vegetable stock

2 cans chopped tomatoes,
   15 oz (410 g) each

1 tablespoon tomato purée

5 fl oz (150 ml) ⅔ cup
   red wine

2 bay leaves

2 sprigs of marjoram

½ teaspoon smoked paprika

2 garlic cloves, crushed and
   chopped

8 shallots

10 oz (300 g) baby carrots,
   scrubbed

10 oz (300 g) new potatoes,
   scrubbed

3 celery stalks, cut into chunks

4 oz (100 g) runner/flat
   beans, chopped

2 oz (50 g) curly kale or
   spring greens, coarsely
   chopped

sea salt and freshly ground
   black pepper

Trim any excess fat from the lamb. Heat the oil in a large
flameproof casserole or saucepan, add the lamb and cook
briefly until browned all over. Depending on the size of the
pan, you may have to do this in batches.

Return all the meat to the pan, sprinkle with a fine
dusting of flour, mix well, and repeat until all the flour has
been incorporated. Add the vegetable stock, tomatoes, tomato
purée, wine, herbs, paprika, garlic, and shallots. Mix well and
bring to the boil. Reduce the heat and simmer gently for 1
hour, stirring from time to time. Add salt and pepper to taste.
(If making in advance, prepare up to this point, let cool, then
chill overnight.)

Add the carrots, potatoes, and celery and cook for
15 minutes. Add the beans and curly kale or greens and stir
gently. Cover with a lid and cook for a further 5 minutes, then
serve with garlic bread.

Sage-stuffed pork fillet with lentils

This meal would be fit to serve in many restaurants and yet is very simple. Pork tenderloin is a much under-used cut, but it is so quick and easy to cook. People seem to worry a great deal about pork being undercooked or tough, but follow the instructions and it will always be cooked through and moist.

SERVES 8

2 pork tenderloins, about 14 oz (375 g) each

leaves from a large bunch of sage

8 thin slices prosciutto

8 oz (250 g) 1½ cups Puy/brown lentils

6 scallions/spring onions, sliced

3 tablespoons olive oil

1 tablespoon red wine

3⅓ fl oz (100 ml) ½ cup sour cream

1 lb (500 g) roasted red bell peppers in a bottle, drained and cut into strips

a bunch of chives, chopped

sea salt and freshly ground black pepper

Preheat the oven to 180°C (350°F) Gas 4.

Trim the pork fillets of any excess fat and, using a long, thin knife, pierce each tenderloin lengthwise through the middle. Push the sage leaves into the slit and, using the handle of a wooden spoon, push them further along the slit. Sprinkle the fillets with salt and pepper, then wrap each one in 4 slices of prosciutto.

Brush a roasting pan with oil, add the wrapped tenderloins, and cook in the preheated oven for 35 minutes. Remove, let rest for 5 minutes, then cut into 1-inch (3-cm) thick slices.

Meanwhile, cook the lentils in simmering water for 20 minutes until tender, then drain. Put the scallions/spring onions into a bowl, add the oil, wine, and sour cream, and mix. Add the peppers to the drained lentils and spoon onto serving plates. Top with the pork slices, scallion dressing, and chives, then serve.

Fish and spring greens pie

Everyone loves a creamy fish pie, packed with goodness. Choose whichever white fish your fishmonger has available.

SERVES 6

1 lb (500 g) white fish fillet, such as cod, haddock, halibut, or whiting

1 lb (500 g) trout fillet

8 oz (200 g) uncooked peeled shrimp/prawns

4 oz (100 g) scallops

10 oz (300 g) spring greens or Savoy cabbage, coarsely chopped

2 lbs (1 kg) potatoes, cut into equal pieces

4 tablespoons (50 g) butter

3⅓ fl oz (100 ml) ½ cup milk

sea salt and freshly ground black pepper

SAUCE

1 pint (500 ml) 2 cups milk

3½ oz (100 g) 1 stick butter

1¼ oz (50 g) ⅓ cup all-purpose/plain flour

4 oz (100 g) 1 cup Cheddar cheese, grated

sea salt and freshly ground black pepper

Preheat the oven to 200°C (400°F) Gas 6.

Dry the fish and seafood thoroughly with paper towels. Arrange the spring greens in a large ovenproof dish and put the fish and seafood on top.

Cook the potatoes in a saucepan of boiling, salted water for 20 minutes, or until tender when pierced with a knife. Drain and return to the pan. Mash well, then add the butter, milk, and salt and pepper to taste. Beat well with a wooden spoon, then set aside until needed.

To make the sauce, put the milk into a small saucepan and heat gently until warm. Melt the butter in a separate saucepan and add the flour. Remove from the heat, stir, return to the heat, then add a little of the warm milk. Stir well, then gradually stir in the remaining warm milk until the sauce is smooth. Add the cheese, salt, and pepper, then pour over the fish.

Spoon the mashed potatoes evenly over the top, giving it a scalloped effect. If you want a more traditional look, run a fork over the surface of the potato. Transfer to the preheated oven and bake for 20 minutes, then reduce to 160°C (325°F) Gas 3 and cook for a further 25 minutes.

Seared scallops with crushed potatoes

With their sweet flesh and subtle hint of the sea, scallops are a real treat.
Truffle oil, though expensive, is used sparingly and transforms this dish into
something special. If you don't have any truffle oil, use a flavored
oil of your choice.

SERVES 4

12 large sea scallops, corals
    removed

1 tablespoon extra virgin
    olive oil

sea salt and freshly ground
    black pepper

CRUSHED POTATOES

1 lb (500 g) new potatoes,
    peeled

1 tablespoon extra virgin
    olive oil

1 oz (25 g) ¼ cup pitted
    black olives, chopped

1 tablespoon chopped fresh
    flat-leaf parsley

a few drops of truffle oil
    (optional)

Cook the potatoes in a saucepan of lightly salted, boiling water
until just tender. Drain well and return to the pan. Lightly
crush them with a fork, leaving them still a little chunky. Add
the olive oil, olives, parsley, and a few drops of truffle oil, if
using. Season with salt and pepper and stir well.

Put the scallops in a bowl, add the olive oil, salt, and
pepper. Toss to coat. Sear the scallops on a preheated stove-top
grill pan for 1 minute on each side (don't overcook or they
will be tough). Remove to a plate and let them rest briefly.

Put a pile of crushed potatoes onto each plate, lay the
scallops on top, and sprinkle with a few extra drops of truffle
oil, if using.

Roasted salmon wrapped in prosciutto

What makes this dish such a joy is that you will have no last-minute dramas with the fish falling to pieces, because the prosciutto not only adds flavor and crispness, it also parcels up the salmon.

SERVES 4

4 thin slices Fontina cheese, rind removed

4 salmon fillets, 8 oz (175 g) each, skinned

4 bay leaves

8 thin slices prosciutto

sea salt and freshly ground black pepper

ZUCCHINI RIBBONS AND PASTA

8 oz (200 g) dried pappardelle pasta

8 oz (200 g) zucchini/ courgettes, very thinly sliced lengthwise

finely grated zest and freshly squeezed juice of 1 unwaxed lemon

2 tablespoons extra virgin olive oil

a bunch of chives, finely chopped

Preheat the oven to 200°C (400°F) Gas 6. Lightly oil a baking tray.

Trim the Fontina slices to fit on top of the salmon fillets. Put a bay leaf on top of each fillet, then a slice of the Fontina. Wrap 2 slices of prosciutto around each piece of salmon, so that it is completely covered.

Transfer to the baking tray and cook in the preheated oven for 10–15 minutes, depending on the thickness of the salmon fillets.

Meanwhile, cook the pasta in a large saucepan of boiling, salted water until *al dente*, or according to the directions on the packet. Add the zucchini/courgette slices to the pasta for the final 3 minutes of cooking.

Put the lemon zest and juice in a bowl, add the oil, and mix. Add the chives, salt, and pepper. Drain the pasta and courgettes and return them to the pan. Add the lemon juice mixture and toss to coat. Serve with the roasted salmon.

Mediterranean fish stew

I love fish stew, and this easy, stress-free recipe makes a fantastic meal (I have used it many times). Don't forget to provide a few empty dishes for discarded shells and some bowls of warm water for washing fingers.

SERVES 8

5 tablespoons (75 ml) ⅓ cup olive oil

3 garlic cloves, chopped

2 onions, chopped

2 leeks or onions, chopped

3 celery stalks, sliced

1 fennel bulb, trimmed and sliced

1 tablespoon all-purpose/ plain flour

1 bay leaf

a sprig of thyme

a generous pinch of saffron threads

3 cans chopped tomatoes, 15 oz (410 g) each

4 pints (2 litres) 8 cups fish stock

2 lbs (1 kg) monkfish tail, cut into 8 pieces

1 lb (500 g) mussels in shells, scrubbed

8 scallops

8 uncooked shrimp/prawns, shell on

a bunch of flat-leaf parsley, chopped

sea salt and freshly ground black pepper

crusty bread, to serve

Heat the oil in a large saucepan and add the chopped garlic, onion, leeks, celery, and fennel. Cook over a low to medium heat for 10 minutes until all the ingredients have softened. Sprinkle in the flour and stir well. Add the bay leaf, thyme, saffron threads, chopped tomatoes, and fish stock. Season with salt and pepper. Bring to a boil, then simmer gently for 25 minutes.

Add the monkfish, mussels, scallops, and shrimp/prawns to the pan. Cover the saucepan with a lid, and simmer very gently for 6 minutes. Remove the pan from the heat and set aside, with the lid on, for 4 minutes. Add the chopped parsley and serve the stew in warmed bowls with plenty of warm, crusty bread.

Butternut and goat cheese gratin

A beautifully balanced vegetarian main course, perfect for an evening at home with friends. Parsnips and ginger together may be a surprising combination but they are a compelling and interesting variation on traditional mashed potato.

SERVES 6

4 lbs (2 kg) butternut
   squash or pumpkin

4 tablespoons (60 ml) ¼ cup
   olive oil

4 tablespoons (50 g)
   unsalted butter

12 oz (350 g) canned corn
   kernels, drained

½ teaspoon freshly grated
   nutmeg

2 garlic cloves, crushed

fresh thyme leaves off the
   stalk

sea salt and freshly ground
   black pepper

5 oz (140 g) 3 cups fresh
   bread crumbs

4 oz (100 g) aged/firm
   goat cheese, grated

PARSNIP MASH

1½ lbs (750 g) parsnips,
   coarsely chopped

1 tablespoon safflower/
   sunflower oil

1 teaspoon ground ginger

10 fl oz (300 ml) 1¼ cups
   heavy/double cream

sea salt and freshly ground
   black pepper

Preheat the oven to 200°C (400°F) Gas 6.

Put the squash in an ovenproof dish with 1 tablespoon of the olive oil, the butter in pieces, corn, nutmeg, garlic, thyme, salt, and pepper.

To make the topping, mix the bread crumbs, goat cheese, and remaining oil in a bowl, then sprinkle over the squash. Cover with foil and bake in the preheated oven for 40 minutes. Remove the foil and cook for a further 15 minutes until golden brown on top.

Meanwhile, make the mash. Put the parsnips on a baking tray and sprinkle with salt, safflower/sunflower oil, and ginger. Roast in the preheated oven for about 20 minutes until the parsnips are tender. Transfer to a food processor, add the cream, and blend until smooth. Add salt and pepper to taste. Transfer to a second ovenproof glass dish, cover with foil, and heat in the oven for 10 minutes. Serve the gratin with the parsnip mash.

Wild mushroom risotto

Risottos always go down well and, once you've got the hang of them, they are incredibly easy to make. Use wild mushrooms in season or cremini/chestnut mushrooms with some dried porcini when they're not available.

SERVES 4

7 oz (200 g) wild mushrooms or 9 oz (250 g) cremini/chestnut mushrooms and 1 oz (25 g) dried porcini, soaked for 15 minutes in warm water

2 tablespoons light olive oil

3¼ oz (90 g) 6 tablespoons unsalted butter

1 small–medium onion, finely chopped

10½ oz (300 g) 1½ cups arborio or carnaroli risotto rice

2½ pints (1.2 litres) 5 cups homemade chicken stock or stock made with vegetable bouillon powder

¼ pint (125 ml) ½ cup dry white wine

3 heaped tablespoons Parmesan cheese, plus extra to serve

salt and freshly ground black pepper

Clean the fresh mushrooms by lightly wiping with a damp cloth. Slice them thinly. If you're using porcini, drain and slice them too.

Heat a medium skillet/frying pan, add 1 tablespoon of oil and 3 tablespoons (40 g) of the butter, and briefly fry the fresh mushrooms until lightly browned. Heat the remaining oil and 1½ tablespoons (25 g) of the remaining butter in a large saucepan, then add the onion. Stir and cook over a medium heat, for about 3 minutes, then tip in the rice and stir. Let it cook for about 3 minutes without coloring, stirring occasionally so that it doesn't catch on the pan.

Meanwhile, heat the stock in another saucepan until it is almost boiling and leave over low heat. Pour the wine into the rice. It will sizzle and evaporate almost immediately. Add the dried mushrooms, if using, then gradually add the stock, a ladleful at a time, stirring the risotto in between and cooking it until the liquid has almost been absorbed. Then add the next lot of stock and repeat until the rice is nice and creamy but still has a little "bite" to it. This will take about 20 minutes.

About 5 minutes before the end of the cooking time, stir in the sautéed mushrooms, leaving a few for garnishing. When the risotto is ready, stir in the remaining butter and Parmesan, and season to taste. Leave the pan covered for a few minutes while you reheat the remaining mushrooms. Serve the risotto in bowls topped with a few mushrooms and some extra Parmesan.

· ACCOMPANIMENTS ·

Pomme purée

This is the decadent French way of cooking mash.

SERVES 6

2¼ lbs (1 kg) red-skinned
   potatoes, such as Desirée
   or Wilja

1½ fl oz (50 ml)
   3 tablespoons
   heavy/double cream

2½–3⅓ fl oz (75–100 ml)
   ¼–⅓ cup whole milk

2½ tablespoons (75 g)
   unsalted butter, cut into
   cubes and at room
   temperature

sea salt and freshly ground
   black pepper

Peel the potatoes and cut them into quarters or eighths (about half the size you would cut them for normal mash). Put them in a saucepan, pour over boiling water, add 1 teaspoon salt, and bring back to the boil. Turn down the heat and simmer gently for about 12–15 minutes until you can easily pierce them with a skewer. Drain them in a colander, then return them to the pan over very low heat and leave them for a minute or two to dry off.

Mix the cream and milk together and heat until just below boiling point in a microwave or separate saucepan. Tip the potatoes back into the colander, then pass them through a potato ricer back into the pan. Pour in half the cream mixture and beat with a wooden spoon, then gradually beat in the remaining cream mixture and the butter. Season to taste with salt and pepper.

Carrot and spinach butter mash

If you wish, the carrots can be cooked a little in advance and kept
warm in the oven, until you are ready to add the spinach just
before serving.

SERVES 8

1 lb (400 g) carrots, chopped

6 tablespoons (75 g) butter

10 oz (300 g) spinach,
    chopped

sea salt and freshly ground
    black pepper

Cook the carrots in a saucepan of boiling, salted water for
30 minutes, or until tender. Drain well, reserving the cooking
water for the gravy. Return the carrots to the pan and put over
low heat. Steam off the excess water, stirring frequently, for
2 minutes.

Remove from the heat, add the butter, salt, and pepper, and
mash well. Add the spinach and stir for 2 minutes, until wilted.

Garlic sautéed green beans

It may seem odd not to cook the beans in a pan of water, but
with this method the beans take on a wonderful buttery, garlic flavor,
while keeping their crunchy texture.

SERVES 8

2 garlic cloves, crushed and
    finely chopped

2 tablespoons (25 g) butter

2 tablespoons olive oil

8 oz (200 g) runner/flat
    beans, trimmed and cut
    into 3 pieces each

8 oz (200 g) fine green
    beans, trimmed

8 oz (200 g) sugar snap
    peas, trimmed

freshly ground black pepper

Put the garlic, butter, and oil into a large saucepan and
heat gently. When hot, add all the beans and sugar snap
peas and cook, stirring frequently, for 5 minutes until they
are tender but still slightly crisp. Sprinkle with plenty of
black pepper and serve.

· DESSERTS ·

Grape and lemon mascarpone tart

This is a really simple dessert that you can make with a ready-made pastry base. A gorgeous Italian lemon liqueur gives a sharp edge to the creamy mascarpone.

SERVES 6–8

8 oz (230 g) ready-made puff pastry dough, thawed if frozen

2 large eggs, separated

2 tablespoons superfine/unrefined caster sugar, plus 1 teaspoon for sprinkling

8-oz (250-g) tub mascarpone cheese

2½ tablespoons Limoncello (lemon liqueur)

8 oz (250 g) white seedless or halved and seeded grapes, rinsed and dried

8 oz (250 g) red seedless or halved and seeded grapes, rinsed and dried

1 teaspoon confectioners'/icing sugar

Preheat the oven to 200°C (400°F) Gas 6. Lightly grease a large, square, or rectangular baking tray.

Take the pastry out of the fridge and let it rest for 20 minutes. Unroll and lift carefully onto the baking tray. Trim around the edge to make a 11-inch (28-cm) round.

Lightly whisk the egg whites and brush a thin layer onto the pastry. Sprinkle with 1 teaspoon superfine/caster sugar, then use a fork to prick the pastry all over. Bake for 10–12 minutes until puffy and brown. Leave to cool while you make the topping.

Tip the mascarpone cheese into a bowl and gradually work in the Limoncello. Using an electric hand-held whisk, beat the egg yolks with the remaining superfine sugar until pale, thick, and creamy. Gently fold the mascarpone mixture into the eggs until thoroughly blended.

Transfer the cooled pastry base to a large serving plate or tray. Spread over the mascarpone mixture with a spatula, taking it almost up to the edges. Scatter the grapes on top to get a nice mix of colors.

Sift over the confectioners'/icing sugar and serve straight away, or chill the tart for a couple of hours, then sprinkle with confectioners' sugar when ready to serve.

Raspberry and brown sugar meringues

I love the little explosions of fruit in the middle of these meringues. They won't keep as long as conventional meringues, so do eat them within two to three hours of making them.

MAKES 16 MERINGUES

4 large egg whites, at room temperature

5¼ oz (150 g) ¼ cup superfine/unrefined caster sugar

1¼ oz (50 g) ¼ cup light brown muscovado sugar, sifted

7 oz (200 g) 1½ cups frozen raspberries, unthawed

Preheat the oven to 150°C (300°F) Gas 2. Lightly grease 2 large, non-stick baking trays with flavorless oil or line with baking parchment.

Put the egg whites in a large, clean grease-free bowl and start to whisk them (easiest with an electric hand-held whisk). Increase the speed as they begin to froth up, moving the whisk around the bowl, until they just hold a peak (about 2–3 minutes). Gradually add the superfine/caster sugar a teaspoonful at a time, beating the meringue well between each addition. When half the superfine sugar has been incorporated, add the rest of the superfine sugar a spoonful at a time. Gradually add the brown sugar, then gently fold in the frozen raspberries, ensuring that they are fully coated by the meringue.

Using 2 dessertspoons, carefully spoon the meringues onto the prepared baking trays. Place in the preheated oven and immediately reduce the heat to 140°C (275°F) Gas 1. Bake for 1¼ hours until the meringues are firm. Turn off the heat and leave the meringues to cool in the oven.

You can refrigerate the meringues for up to 3 hours, lightly covered with plastic wrap, before serving.

Roast pears with sweet wine and honey

Roasting pears in wine transforms them from everyday fruit into a light but luxurious dessert. The trick is to use an inexpensive wine for cooking and a better wine of the same type to serve with it.

SERVES 6

*freshly squeezed juice of
1 lemon (about
3 tablespoons)*

*9 just-ripe, small Conference
pears*

*3 tablespoons (50 g) butter,
softened*

3 tablespoons fragrant honey

*6 fl oz (175 ml) ⅔ cup
Premières Côtes de
Bordeaux or late-harvested
Sauvignon or Semillon*

1¾ oz (50 g) ⅓ cup pine nuts

*2 teaspoons superfine/
unrefined caster sugar*

*6¾ fl oz (200 ml) ¼ cup
heavy/double cream*

*2 teaspoons vanilla sugar or
½ teaspoon vanilla extract
and 2 teaspoons superfine
sugar*

Preheat the oven to 190°C (375°F) Gas 5. Grease a large roasting pan or ovenproof dish (big enough to take the pears in a single layer) well with butter.

Strain the lemon juice into a small bowl. Cut each pear in half, peel it, and cut away the core. Dip it in the lemon juice to stop it discoloring. Place it cut-side upward in the roasting pan or dish. Arrange the pears so that they fit snugly in one layer. Put a knob of butter in the center of each half. Drizzle the pears with the honey and pour over the leftover lemon juice and the wine.

Bake in the preheated oven for about 50 minutes–1 hour, turning the pears halfway through. If the pears produce a lot of juice turn the heat up to 200°C (400°F) Gas 6 to concentrate the juices and form a syrup. Remove from the oven and let cool for about 20 minutes. (You can part-cook the dish for about 30 minutes a couple of hours before dinner, then finish cooking it once you sit down at table, allowing it to cool during the entrée.)

Meanwhile, toast the pine nuts lightly in a skillet/frying pan, shaking them occasionally until they start to brown. Sprinkle over the superfine/caster sugar and continue to cook until the sugar melts and caramelizes. Sweeten the cream with the vanilla sugar and heat until lukewarm. Arrange 3 pear halves on each plate, trickle over about a tablespoon of warm cream, and scatter over the pine nuts.

Hazelnut, chocolate, and cardamom cream

This is delicious with a glass of Frangelico (Italian hazelnut liqueur).

SERVES 8

FOR THE PASTRY

5 tablespoons (60 g)
    unsalted butter, softened

3 tablespoons (25 g)
    confectioners'/icing sugar

3½ oz (100 g)
    3 tablespoons hazelnuts

4¼ oz (125 g) 1 cup
    all-purpose/
    plain flour, unsifted

1 egg yolk

FOR THE FILLING

10 green cardamom pods

10 fl oz (300 ml) 1¼ cups
    heavy/double cream

7 oz (200 g) premium
    bittersweet/dark chocolate
    (minimum 70% cocoa
    solids), broken into chunks

2 tablespoons (25 g)
    unsalted butter

1 tablespoon unsweetened
    cocoa powder, sifted, to
    decorate

Preheat the oven to 190°C (375°F) Gas 5. Spread the hazelnuts out on a baking tray and toast in the preheated oven for 15 minutes or until lightly browned. Cool, then chop in a food processor or coffee grinder (you may have to do this in batches). Cream the butter with the sifted confectioners'/icing sugar, add 3 tablespoons (40 g) of the hazelnuts, then gradually work in the flour. Beat the egg yolk with 1 tablespoon water and add to the mixture, gradually pulling it into a ball.

Turn out onto a floured board or work surface and roll or press it out gently into a round slightly smaller than a 9-inch (23-cm) fluted pie plate/flan tin. Carefully lower it into the pie plate (don't worry if it breaks) and press it round and up the side until you have formed a pastry case. Chill in the refrigerator for at least half an hour, then prick the base and bake it in the oven for about 15–20 minutes until lightly browned. Let cool.

Meanwhile, crush the cardamoms in a mortar with a pestle or with the end of a rolling pin. Remove the green husks and finely grind the seeds. Add to the cream and gently warm in a saucepan until the surface is just beginning to tremble. (Don't let it boil.) Take off the heat and add the chocolate chunks, butter, and the remaining ground hazelnuts. Set aside to cool, but don't let it get cold. Pour into the pastry case and put in the refrigerator for at least 2 hours. Dust the surface with cocoa powder before serving.

· COCKTAILS ·

Homemade lemonade

You will need a juicer to make this absolutely delicious lemonade—
in fact, it's almost worth buying one just to make it.

MAKES 6–8 GLASSES

5¼ oz (150 g) ¾ cup
superfine/unrefined
caster sugar

4 large juicy unwaxed
lemons, plus 1 extra,
sliced, to garnish

1¾ pints (1 litre) 3½ cups
still or sparkling mineral
water, chilled

a few sprigs of mint

plenty of ice, to serve

Put the sugar in a saucepan with 5¼ fl oz (150 ml) ⅔ cup water. Heat over low heat, stirring until the sugar has completely dissolved, then bring to the boil and boil for 5 minutes without stirring. Take off the heat and leave to cool. Cut 2 of the lemons into small chunks and pass through the feeder tube of a juicer. They should produce about 5¼ fl oz (150 ml) ⅔ cup thick juice. Squeeze the remaining lemons—again, that should yield about 5¼ fl oz (150 ml) ⅔ cup—and add to the other juice. Stir in the sugar syrup you've made.

Chill the lemon concentrate until ready to use. Either pour into a large pitcher full of ice and pour in an equal amount of chilled still or sparkling mineral water, or pour a couple of shots of lemonade into a tumbler full of ice and top up with chilled mineral water. Garnish with lemon slices and sprigs of mint.

VARIATION

Raspberry lemonade

Purée (in a food processor or force through a nylon-mesh sieve) 5¼ oz (150 g) 1 cup of fresh or frozen raspberries and sweeten with 2 tablespoons sugar syrup (see recipe above). Stir into the lemonade base and dilute as described. Decorate with lemon slices and a few whole raspberries.

Classic dry martini

The Classic Dry Martini has long been considered the ultimate in sophistication and elegance. Its roots date back as far as the 1840s, where it is believed to have been served at a bar in Martinez, California.

SERVES 6

2 fl oz (50 ml) gin

a dash of dry vermouth

green olive, to garnish

Using a mixing glass, chill the gin and vermouth over ice, and pour into a frosted martini glass. Garnish with a green olive.

Classic margarita

All you need to create a margarita is good-quality tequila, lime, and orange-flavored liqueur. Yet within the boundaries of these ingredients you can make your drink taste quite different. The type of tequila, the choice of sour, the brand of sweetener, and the ratio of all three influence the final flavor. There is no such thing as the perfect margarita and the only person who can judge the levels of perfection is its recipient.

SERVES 1

2 fl oz (50 ml) gold tequila

scant fl oz (20 ml) triple sec

1 fl oz (25 ml) fresh lime juice

lime wheel, to garnish

salt (for the glass)

Add all the ingredients to a shaker filled with ice. Shake sharply and strain into a salt-rimmed, chilled margarita glass. Garnish with a lime wheel.

For frozen margaritas, add all the ingredients to a blender, add one scoop of crushed ice, and blend for 20 seconds. Pour into a margarita coupette, and garnish with a lime wheel.

Bloody mary

The Bloody Mary has been a renowned hangover cure or pick-me-up for years. Curing hangovers can be painless and should be enjoyable, too. They are an aspect of bartending that cannot be ignored—and, in a truly biblical way, what the bartender giveth, so shall he take away.

SERVES 1

2 fl oz (50 ml) vodka

8 fl oz (200 ml) tomato juice

2 grinds of black pepper

2 dashes of Worcestershire sauce

2 dashes of Tabasco sauce

2 dashes of fresh lemon juice

1 barspoon horseradish

1 celery stick, to garnish

Shake all the ingredients over ice and strain into a highball glass filled with ice. Garnish with a celery stick. (These measurements depend on personal tastes for spices.)

Vodka collins

Try the Vodka Collins for a sharp, zingy, thirst quencher on a hot day. Be warned, it's easy to forget there is alcohol in the drink!

SERVES 1

1¼ fl oz (50 ml) vodka

¾ fl oz (20 ml) fresh lemon juice

½ fl oz (15 ml) sugar syrup

club soda, to top up

lemon slice, to garnish

Build the ingredients into a highball glass filled with ice. Stir gently and garnish with a lemon slice. Serve with two straws.

Mint mojito

Zesty and refreshing, a mojito is the perfect summer drink to refresh and revive. Before serving, strain through a fine-mesh sieve to remove all the pieces of chopped mint (it's the mint juice that gives it such an amazing color).

SERVES 1

2¼ fl oz (60 ml) ¼ cup white rum

freshly squeezed juice of 1 lime

1 tablespoon sugar or sugar syrup

leaves from a large bunch of mint

ice cubes

sparkling mineral water (optional)

mint sprigs and lime zest, to serve

Put the rum, lime juice, sugar or sugar syrup, mint leaves, and ice cubes in a blender and zap well until mixed. Strain the blended mixture into a glass half-filled with ice cubes. Serve straight or topped up with sparkling mineral water, with a sprig of mint and a curl of lime zest.

The perfect manhattan

The naming of Manhattan Island has an anecdotal history that links it with the cocktail. "Manhachtanienck," which roughly translates as "the island where we became intoxicated," was so named in the early seventeenth century by Lenape Indians after drinking a dark spirit.

SERVES 1

2 fl oz (50 ml) rye whiskey

1 fl oz (25 ml) sweet vermouth

a dash of orange (e.g. Angostura) bitters

orange zest, to garnish

Add the ingredients to a mixing glass filled with ice (make sure all ingredients are very cold) and stir the mixture until chilled. Strain into a frosted martini glass, add the garnish, and serve.

Pairing Food and Wine

There is only one hard and fast rule for you to bear in mind when matching wine with food, and that is: Don't Be Afraid. Experiment! Trial and error really is the only way to find that perfect pairing where wine and food combine in harmony, each enhancing the other.

Generally speaking, the lighter the dish, the lighter the wine should be; the heavier the dish, the heavier the wine. But try anything once, and if you get it wrong, stop. You will know better next time.

There are, of course, some classic combinations that are hard to beat: a chilled bottle of Muscadet Sur Lie with a plate of oysters, for example, a fine red burgundy with a dish of boeuf bourgignon (the beef is cooked in that wine after all) or an inky black Cahors with a steaming bowl of cassoulet, but such pairings are not etched in tablets of stone. Everyone's taste differs, and while you should always bear in mind the experience of those who have trodden this path before you, the only way to find out what you like is to try it for yourself.

Don't be scared of serving red wine with fish, for example; you will soon learn whether the pairing works to your taste or not. Although it is true that most red wines are made to taste unpleasantly metallic by fish or seafood dishes, there are some combinations that work perfectly—Oregon Pinot Noir with salmon or tuna steak for example. Similarly, why restrict the sweet wine to accompanying dessert? A rich and luscious Sauternes, late harvest Australian Semillon, or Muscat de Beaumes-de-Venise goes just as well with pâté de foie gras at the start of a meal as it does with a strong blue cheese at the end.

In the Old World, wines have had centuries in which to evolve in such a way that they match local cuisine perfectly and vice versa. It is no accident that the white wines of the Loire match seafood so well; that there is nothing better with Greek food than that acquired taste, Retsina; that Tokay Pinot Gris goes so well with a choucroute

Alsacienne. The New World does not have this history of wine and food combinations, which perhaps allows it to be a bit more adventurous and daring.

The pairings listed below should be considered as no more than suggestions and ideas to set you on your way; wine was created to accompany food, and you will be surprised at some of the unlikely combinations that succeed. Be brave and enjoy.

APERITIFS

Champagne or sparkling wine, if the occasion demands it, otherwise a well-chilled Fino or Manzanilla sherry will kick-start the most jaded of appetites. If you're bored with white wine, try a Beaujolais or red Sancerre straight from the fridge.

BARBECUED MEAT

A red with a bit of zing is required here, such as a New World Zinfandel, Pinotage, or Australian Shiraz, or perhaps a meaty Rhône or southern French country wine.

BEEF

BEEF STEWS AND CASSEROLES A robust red such as a Côte Rôtie or Hermitage from the Rhône, an Australian Shiraz or a top-quality Rioja. Or try a big, oak-aged Chardonnay from Burgundy or Australia.
COLD ROAST BEEF (See Cold Cuts)
COTTAGE PIE A full-bodied Zinfandel or Côtes du Rhône.
HAMBURGERS A young, fruity Chianti or Beaujolais or Spanish Tempranillo would work well, as would a Chilean Merlot or Cabernet Sauvignon. Or try a full-bodied

white instead, such as a Viognier or Australian oaked Semillon.
ROAST BEEF Any good red wine might be the obvious choice, but a good quality Pinot Gris from Alsace will have the weight and the depth of flavor to make a very decent substitute.
STEAK A New World Cabernet Sauvignon is hard to beat.
STEAK AND KIDNEY PIE Something hearty like a Rhône, Australian Shiraz, or Italian Barolo.

BISCUITS

Medium-dry madeira such as Bual or Rainwater or a tawny port. An Amontillado sherry or a medium-dry Vouvray.

BRUNCH

Champagne or sparkling wine if your stomach can cope, a Bloody Mary if it can't. (And don't forget that the perfect Bloody Mary has a dash of Amontillado sherry added to it.)

CANAPÉS

Sparkling wine, chilled Fino or Manzanilla sherry, or any light, dry white wine.

CASSOULET

This dish is always best accompanied by
a French country wine such as Cahors,
Madiran, or Corbières.

CHEESE

BLUE CHEESE (such as Stilton, St. Agur) An
intensely sweet Sauternes or Beerenauslese
can't be bettered. Vintage port is traditional,
but why not try an Italian Barbera or Chilean
Cabernet Sauvignon instead?

CHEESE ON TOAST Something young and
full-bodied such as Chilean Merlot. Or a dry
white Bordeaux or similar Rhône.

GOAT CHEESE White wine seems to
work best: a bone-dry one, such as a classy
Sauvignon Blanc from New Zealand or the
Loire, or an intensely sweet one, such as a
Sauternes or Vouvray.

HARD CHEESES (such as Cheddar, Edam,
Gloucester, Gouda) A middling quality claret
or tawny port.

SOFT CHEESES (such as Camembert and
Brie) Almost any red wine will do, but
nothing fancy. Surprisingly, an unoaked
Chardonnay from Chablis, say, or the New
World, often makes a better partner to such
cheeses than a red wine would.

STRONG CHEESES (such as Roquefort,
Munster) A late harvest Gewürztraminer
from Alsace, or an Icewine from Canada—
both served well-chilled—will make you
wonder why you never tried such a pairing
before. You could also try a rich madeira or
Ruby port.

CHICKEN

CHICKEN IN CREAMY SAUCES Such
dishes need something with a bit of character,
like an Alsace Pinot Gris or a New Zealand
Sauvignon Blanc.

CHICKEN LIVER PATE A dry white from
Burgundy or Bordeaux, or even a Viognier.

CHICKEN PIE Try a Chilean Cabernet
Sauvignon or Merlot.

COLD CHICKEN For a red, choose
something light, a Beaujolais perhaps, or red
Loire, or any white wine with a bit of oomph,
such as a white Rhône or a white Rioja.

COQ AU VIN Red burgundy is the obvious
(and most authentic) choice, otherwise a
good New World Pinot Noir.

ROAST CHICKEN Almost any red wine—
a full-flavored white wine such as a New
World Chardonnay or mature white
burgundy will also hit the spot.
CHILLI CON CARNE Nothing fancy, a
simple Chianti or Valpolicella is best, or an
Argentinian Malbec.

CHINESE FOOD

White wine for preference, such as anything
from Alsace, a medium-dry German
Riesling, or a Californian Chardonnay, but
you could do worse than a New World
Pinot or Beaujolais.

CHOCOLATE (see Desserts)

COLD CUTS

A spread of ham, roast beef, pork pies,
and salami is best matched with a young
fruity red from Bordeaux or the Rhône.
But go easy on the chutney and pickled
onions, which are death to red wine. Full-
flavored and characterful white wines can
also work, such as Alsace Pinot Gris,
California Chardonnay, and Australian
Semillon or Chardonnay.

COTTAGE PIE (See Beef)

DESSERTS

CAKE Oloroso or Cream sherry.
CHOCOLATE PUDDING The only wines

that can really stand up to chocolate are the
Black Muscats and Orange Muscats of
California and Australia.
CUSTARDS Sauternes or Monbazillac.
FRESH FRUIT Fruit can be tricky, so
best stick to a sweet Coteaux du Layon
or Vouvray.
FRUIT TARTS German or Austrian
Beerenauslese, or a late harvest Alsace
Gewürztraminer.
ICE CREAM AND SORBETS Take a
break from the wine here, and come back
to it afterward.
STRAWBERRIES AND CREAM A sweet
Vouvray is ideal, or try a sweet sparkler like
Asti Spumante.

DUCK

GRILLED DUCK BREASTS Zinfandel or an
oaky Rioja.
ROAST DUCK Pair this with a full-bodied
red such as Barolo, Châteauneuf-du-Pape,
Hermitage, or Australian Shiraz. However,
if you prefer a white wine, an aromatic
Viognier, top-quality Chablis, or Alsace is
needed here.

EGG DISHES

Eggs aren't the ideal partners for wine, but
a plate of scrambled eggs and smoked
salmon always seems to demand champagne
or top-quality sparkling wine.

FISH

FISH AND CHIPS Why not opt for champagne? Otherwise you could try a crisp white such as Chablis, or even, given that this is such a traditional English dish, a dry English wine.

FISH IN CREAMY SAUCES Such dishes are well-partnered by Riesling—from Australia, Alsace, or Germany.

BOUILLABAISSE Any dry wine from the Loire—a Pouilly-Fumé or Sancerre if you are in funds, a Muscadet or Sauvignon de Touraine if you are not.

FISH PATE An aromatic Viognier or an Alsace Riesling would be perfect.

FISH PIE Try a Sauvignon Blanc from New Zealand or Chile, or a new-wave Spanish Albariño.

FRITTO MISTO A light, dry Italian such as Verdicchio, Orvieto, or Frascati.

GRAVADLAX Chablis, New World Chardonnay, or Viognier.

GRILLED SALMON Chablis, white burgundy, or New World Chardonnay. It may surprise you, but some fish dishes do go well with red wine, and an Oregon Pinot Noir would be perfect here.

GRILLED SOLE OR PLAICE Such a simple dish will allow any top-quality wine to show off, such as the best white burgundy or Chablis you can lay your hands on.

GRILLED TROUT Try an English wine; oh, go on!

GRILLED TURBOT AND TUNA A white Rhône or an Australian Riesling.

RED MULLET A well-chilled red Loire or a classy dry rosé.

SMOKED EEL, MACKEREL, AND SALMON Australian Semillon or Alsace Gewürztraminer.

SMOKED HADDOCK OR COD White Rhône or full-bodied Chardonnay.

TUNA STEAKS Try a top-class Beaujolais or even a New World Pinot Noir.

FOIE GRAS

Top-quality sweet wine such as Sauternes, Alsace Vendange Tardive, or Canadian Icewine. Otherwise a dry Viognier.

GAME

Meats such as grouse, hare, partridge, pheasant, pigeon, rabbit, venison, or wild boar, whether roasted or casseroled need hefty, big-boned wines such as California Cabernet Sauvignon, Barolo, a fine Rhône, or Rioja.

GOOSE

This deserves a decent claret or a red burgundy. For a white wine, something big and highly-flavoured is needed, such as an Alsace Pinot Gris or an Hermitage Blanc. You might even consider an off-dry Riesling such as a German Spätlese.

GREEK FOOD

Retsina is the obvious choice for the

taramasalata and calamari, but since it is something of an acquired taste you might prefer a Muscadet or an Italian Chardonnay. Stick to white for the first courses and then a rustic red from Greece, southern France, Lebanon, or north Africa for the moussaka and lamb kebabs.

HAM (See Cold Cuts)

INDIAN FOOD

Beer is the obvious choice, but failing that, try a well-chilled light red such as Beaujolais, or an ice-cold medium-dry Vouvray or an off-dry Orvieto.

LAMB

LAMB CHOPS OR CUTLETS Any flavorsome red will work well here, an Australian Cabernet-Shiraz blend perhaps, a Rioja Gran Reserva, or a classy Merlot- based claret.
ROAST LAMB This classic dish deserves a fine red Bordeaux or New World Cabernet Sauvignon. Something full-flavoured but dry is needed if you are eschewing red wine, like an Hermitage Blanc.
SHEPHERD'S PIE A Crozes-Hermitage, Côtes du Rhône, or California Zinfandel.

LIVER

CALVES' LIVER AND ONIONS The Viennese and Venetians may fight over who invented this dish, but Italian reds such as

Bardolino, Valpolicella, or Chianti are the best accompaniments.

MEXICAN FOOD

A spicy Zinfandel is needed here, or a peppery Rhône such as St. Joseph or Cornas. For whites, try Sauvignon Blancs from Chile, California, or New Zealand.

NORTH AFRICAN FOOD

A Moroccan or Algerian red wine if you can find one, or the excellent Château Musar from the Lebanon. For whites, stick to full-bodied wines from the Rhône or the New World.

NUTS

Choose a Madeira or tawny port.

OLIVES

Dry sherry works best of all.

PASTA

WITH BOLOGNESE SAUCE Any Italian red, but ideally a Chianti Classico.
WITH NEAPOLITAN SAUCE Ditto, but with Barbera as the first choice.
WITH SEAFOOD SAUCE Almost any white wine from Italy, such as Orvieto, Frascati, Soave, or Verdicchio.
WITH PESTO SAUCE The same as for pasta with seafood sauce, although simple unoaked Chardonnay works well too.

and uncomplicated will do, unless the pizza is smothered in anchovies.

PORK

LOIN OF PORK A good Pinot Noir won't let you down, but if you want white, an Australian Semillon also works well.
ROAST PORK Any good red wine goes well with roast pork, but, just for the fun of it, why not try one from Portugal or New Zealand? Any full-bodied white wine will do, too.

PATES AND TERRINES

It depends on what they are made from, but any smooth, soft red should do.

PICNICS

If taking red wine to a picnic, open it beforehand and recork it, or even decant it and rebottle it. (It means that you can taste it beforehand to check that it is okay and clear of sediment, and that you don't have to worry about forgetting the corkscrew.) As for whites, a well-chilled French country wine such as a Côtes de Gascogne if there are lots of you, but treat yourselves to vintage champagne if there are only the two of you.

PIZZA

For authenticity, you really should have an Italian red, but in truth almost anything red

PROSCIUTTO WITH MELON

Try an Italian white such as Orvieto, Lugana, Frascati, or Verdicchio.

QUICHE/ONION TART

Try something light like an Alsace or Oregon Pinot Noir, or perhaps a Beaujolais or Australian Riesling, or, classically, a white Alsace.

RISOTTO

Any red from Italy or the Loire, or an Italian Pinot Grigio.

SALADS

It depends on the dressing and on what is in the salad, but a light red should certainly do the trick, or try a dry and light white, such as a Muscadet or South American Sauvignon Blanc.

SEAFOOD

CAVIAR Champagne is ideal.

COLD LOBSTER This really demands a first rate white burgundy or New World equivalent.

DRESSED CRAB Dry German Riesling or white Rhône.

GRILLED PRAWNS Any dry white wine.

LOBSTER THERMIDOR This dish gives you the chance to dig out an old white burgundy, top-quality New World Chardonnay, or Hermitage Blanc.

SAUTEED SCALLOPS Dry German or Australian Riesling or New Zealand Sauvignon Blanc.

OYSTERS Try any of the following: Chablis, Sancerre, Pouilly-Fumé, or Black Velvet (champagne and draught Guinness, half and half, in a pint tankard).

MOULES ET FRITES Muscadet, Italian Pinot Grigio, or, best of all, unfiltered Belgian wheat beer.

SHEPHERD'S PIE (See Lamb)

SOUP

A Sercial madeira makes a change from the traditional dry sherry.

SUSHI AND SASHIMI

Sake (served hot) or full-flavored New World Chardonnay.

TAPAS

Nothing goes better with tapas than Manzanilla sherry.

THAI FOOD

Beaujolais or red Loire, or, best of all, a spicy New World or Alsace Gewürztraminer.

TURKEY

ROAST TURKEY This most boring of dishes needs a decent red to take your mind off it.

COLD TURKEY So does this.

VEAL

ROAST VEAL Something soft and mature is best, like an old claret, red burgundy, or Rioja. Otherwise a big, oak-aged Chardonnay from Burgundy or Australia.

VEAL IN CREAM SAUCE Pouilly-Fumé, or Sancerre, or even Alsace Riesling.

VEAL IN MARSALA SAUCE A full-bodied Alsace Pinot Gris works well here, or an Australian Verdelho.

VEGETABLES

ROAST VEGETABLES An oaky Chardonnay from Australia or California is ideal.

ENTERTAINING RECORDS

Entertaining Records
My Address Book

ENTERTAINING RECORDS

This section includes the practical pages. There's
a useful section of record pages, so you can keep notes of your
parties and dinners—the occasion, who you invited, the menu
and wines served. And to complete this chapter, there is a list
of companies and websites that I have found useful when
entertaining, plus space for you to note down your own
favorite contacts, such as caterers, delicatessens, wine suppliers,
stationers, and party planners.

DATE

GUESTS

OCCASION

MENU

WINES

DATE

GUESTS

OCCASION

MENU

WINES

DATE

GUESTS

OCCASION

MENU

WINES

DATE _____

GUESTS _____
_____
_____
_____
_____
_____
_____

OCCASION _____

MENU _____
_____
_____
_____

WINES _____
_____

DATE _____

GUESTS _____
_____
_____
_____
_____
_____
_____
_____

OCCASION _____

MENU _____
_____
_____
_____

WINES _____
_____

DATE _____

GUESTS _____
_____
_____
_____
_____
_____
_____
_____

OCCASION _____

MENU _____
_____
_____
_____

WINES _____
_____

DATE

GUESTS

OCCASION

MENU

WINES

DATE

GUESTS

OCCASION

MENU

WINES

DATE

GUESTS

OCCASION

MENU

WINES

DATE

GUESTS

OCCASION

MENU

WINES

DATE

GUESTS

OCCASION

MENU

WINES

DATE

GUESTS

OCCASION

MENU

WINES

DATE _____

GUESTS _____
_____
_____
_____
_____
_____

OCCASION _____

MENU _____
_____
_____
_____
_____

WINES _____
_____

DATE _____

GUESTS _____
_____
_____
_____
_____
_____

OCCASION _____

MENU _____
_____
_____
_____

WINES _____
_____

DATE _____

GUESTS _____
_____
_____
_____
_____
_____
_____

OCCASION _____

MENU _____
_____
_____
_____
_____

WINES _____
_____

DATE

GUESTS

OCCASION

MENU

WINES

DATE

GUESTS

OCCASION

MENU

WINES

DATE

GUESTS

OCCASION

MENU

WINES

DATE _____

GUESTS _____

_____

_____

_____

_____

_____

_____

OCCASION _____

MENU _____

_____

_____

_____

WINES _____

_____

DATE _____

GUESTS _____

_____

_____

_____

_____

_____

_____

OCCASION _____

MENU _____

_____

_____

_____

WINES _____

DATE _____

GUESTS _____

_____

_____

_____

_____

_____

_____

_____

OCCASION _____

MENU _____

_____

_____

_____

WINES _____

_____

DATE

GUESTS

OCCASION

MENU

WINES

DATE

GUESTS

OCCASION

MENU

WINES

DATE

GUESTS

OCCASION

MENU

WINES

DATE _____

GUESTS _____
_____
_____
_____
_____
_____
_____

OCCASION _____

MENU _____
_____
_____
_____

WINES _____
_____

DATE _____

GUESTS _____
_____
_____
_____
_____
_____
_____

OCCASION _____

MENU _____
_____
_____
_____

WINES _____
_____

DATE _____

GUESTS _____
_____
_____
_____
_____
_____
_____

OCCASION _____

MENU _____
_____
_____
_____

WINES _____

DATE

GUESTS

OCCASION

MENU

WINES

DATE

GUESTS

OCCASION

MENU

WINES

DATE

GUESTS

OCCASION

MENU

WINES

DATE

GUESTS

OCCASION

MENU

WINES

DATE

GUESTS

OCCASION

MENU

WINES

DATE

GUESTS

OCCASION

MENU

WINES

DATE

GUESTS

OCCASION

MENU

WINES

DATE

GUESTS

OCCASION

MENU

WINES

DATE

GUESTS

OCCASION

MENU

WINES

· MY ADDRESS BOOK ·

These are some of my favorite contacts around the world.

MY WEBSITES
www.williamyeoward.com
www.williamyeowardcrystal.com
These give details of my
furniture and crystal collections.

www.cicobooks.com
My books and stationery range
(including invitation and reply
cards, thank-you cards, and
place name cards) are all
available from CICO Books as
well as from good book stores
and stationers.

LONDON
Ideas and Concepts
STEPHEN WOODHAMS
(a capable pair of hands)
07701 095 656

Party Planners
JOHNNY ROXBURGH,
Admirable Crichton
020 7326 3800
www.admirable-crichton.co.uk

ARNO MAASDORP
07098 684 967
www.eatwithyoureyes.net

Food
LINDY, ABSOLUTE TASTE
020 8870 5151
www.absolutetaste.co.uk

MUSTARD
020 7840 5900
www.mustardcatering.com

Flowers
VICTORIA BROTHERSON,
Scarlet and Violet
020 8969 9446

Bunting
THE COTTON BUNTING
COMPANY
01376 329 845

NEW YORK
All the below can be found within
New York City.

Flowers
HELENA LEHANE
+1 212 888 7763

ZEZE
www.zezeflowers.com

PLAZA
www.plazaflowersnyc.com

Event Planners
KARA MINOGUE AND CO
+1 212 665 1441
www.karaminogue.com

Calligrapher
SCRIBE INK CALLIGRAPHY
+1 212 249 1817
www.scribeinkcalligraphy.com

Event Decorations
DEJUAN STROUD
www.dejuanstroud.com

ANTONY TODD
www.antonytoddhome.1stdibs.com

DAVID STARK
www.davidstarkdesign.com

BARBADOS
Email Paul Edwards at
pauledwards@caribsurf.com

Also visit the Gourmet shop in
Holetown.

IBIZA
Email Serena at
serena@deliciouslysortedibiza.
com

MALLORCA
Essential store for all
entertaining tables
BARBARA BERGMAN
AND KLAS KALL
Rialto Living Palma S.L.
C/Sant Felui 3c
07012 Palma de Mallorca
+34 971 713 331
www.rialtoliving.com

Caterer
FLAVOURHOUSE
Belgica 61
E07108 Puero de Soller
+34 650 760 766
+34 971 634 784
cpp@flavourhouse.com

Flowers
CUARTO ROSAS
C/Sant Felie 4
07012 Palma de Mallorca
+34 971 724 232

Fill in your own favorite contacts here

COMPANY

CONTACT

ADDRESS

TEL

EMAIL

WEBSITE

COMPANY

CONTACT

ADDRESS

TEL

EMAIL

WEBSITE

COMPANY

CONTACT

ADDRESS

TEL

EMAIL

WEBSITE

COMPANY

CONTACT

ADDRESS

TEL

EMAIL

WEBSITE

COMPANY

CONTACT

ADDRESS

TEL

EMAIL

WEBSITE

COMPANY

CONTACT

ADDRESS

TEL

EMAIL

WEBSITE

COMPANY

CONTACT

ADDRESS

TEL

EMAIL

WEBSITE

COMPANY

CONTACT

ADDRESS

TEL

EMAIL

WEBSITE

COMPANY

CONTACT

ADDRESS

TEL

EMAIL

WEBSITE

COMPANY

CONTACT

ADDRESS

TEL

EMAIL

WEBSITE

COMPANY

CONTACT

ADDRESS

TEL

EMAIL

WEBSITE

COMPANY

CONTACT

ADDRESS

TEL

EMAIL

WEBSITE

COMPANY

CONTACT

ADDRESS

TEL

EMAIL

WEBSITE

COMPANY

CONTACT

ADDRESS

TEL

EMAIL

WEBSITE

COMPANY

CONTACT

ADDRESS

TEL

EMAIL

WEBSITE

COMPANY

CONTACT

ADDRESS

TEL

EMAIL

WEBSITE

COMPANY

CONTACT

ADDRESS

TEL

EMAIL

WEBSITE

COMPANY

CONTACT

ADDRESS

TEL

EMAIL

WEBSITE

COMPANY

CONTACT

ADDRESS

TEL

EMAIL

WEBSITE

COMPANY

CONTACT

ADDRESS

TEL

EMAIL

WEBSITE

COMPANY

CONTACT

ADDRESS

TEL

EMAIL

WEBSITE

COMPANY

CONTACT

ADDRESS

TEL

EMAIL

WEBSITE

COMPANY

CONTACT

ADDRESS

TEL

EMAIL

WEBSITE

COMPANY

CONTACT

ADDRESS

TEL

EMAIL

WEBSITE

COMPANY

CONTACT

ADDRESS

TEL
EMAIL
WEBSITE

COMPANY

CONTACT

ADDRESS

TEL
EMAIL
WEBSITE

COMPANY

CONTACT

ADDRESS

TEL
EMAIL
WEBSITE

COMPANY

CONTACT

ADDRESS

TEL
EMAIL
WEBSITE

COMPANY

CONTACT

ADDRESS

TEL
EMAIL
WEBSITE

COMPANY

CONTACT

ADDRESS

TEL
EMAIL
WEBSITE

· RECIPE CREDITS ·

Fiona Beckett
Chicken, lemon, and green olive tagine
Roast fillet of beef with soy and butter sauce
Wild mushroom risotto
Pomme purée
Grape and lemon mascarpone tart
Raspberry and brown sugar meringues
Roast pears with sweet wine and honey
Hazelnut, chocolate, and cardamom cream
Homemade lemonade

Maxine Clark
Smoked and fresh salmon terrine

Jane Noraika
Butternut and goat cheese gratin

Elsa Petersen-Schepelern
Mint mojito

Louise Pickford
Seared scallops with crushed potatoes

Ben Reed
Classic dry martini
Classic margarita
Bloody mary
Vodka collins
The perfect manhattan

Fran Warde
Roasted eggplant and prosciutto salad
Lamb navarin
Sage-stuffed pork fillet with puy lentils
Fish and spring greens pie
Roasted salmon wrapped in prosciutto
Mediterranean fish stew
Carrot and spinach butter mash
Garlic sautéed green beans